# SpringerBriefs in Computer Science

SpringerBriefs present concise summaries of cutting-edge research and practical applications across a wide spectrum of fields. Featuring compact volumes of 50 to 125 pages, the series covers a range of content from professional to academic.

Typical topics might include:

- A timely report of state-of-the art analytical techniques
- A bridge between new research results, as published in journal articles, and a contextual literature review
- A snapshot of a hot or emerging topic
- An in-depth case study or clinical example
- A presentation of core concepts that students must understand in order to make independent contributions

Briefs allow authors to present their ideas and readers to absorb them with minimal time investment. Briefs will be published as part of Springer's eBook collection, with millions of users worldwide. In addition, Briefs will be available for individual print and electronic purchase. Briefs are characterized by fast, global electronic dissemination, standard publishing contracts, easy-to-use manuscript preparation and formatting guidelines, and expedited production schedules. We aim for publication 8–12 weeks after acceptance. Both solicited and unsolicited manuscripts are considered for publication in this series.

**Indexing: This series is indexed in Scopus, Ei-Compendex, and zbMATH **

More information about this series at http://www.springer.com/series/10028

Tharrmashastha SAPV · Debajyoti Bera ·
Arpita Maitra · Subhamoy Maitra

# Quantum Algorithms for Cryptographically Significant Boolean Functions

## An IBMQ Experience

 Springer

Tharrmashastha SAPV
Computer Science, Indraprastha Institute
of Information Technology
Delhi, India

Debajyoti Bera
Computer Science, Indraprastha Institute
of Information Technology
Delhi, India

Arpita Maitra
TCG-CREST
Kolkata, India

Subhamoy Maitra
Applied Statistics Unit
Indian Statistical Institute
Kolkata, India

ISSN 2191-5768             ISSN 2191-5776  (electronic)
SpringerBriefs in Computer Science
ISBN 978-981-16-3060-6         ISBN 978-981-16-3061-3  (eBook)
https://doi.org/10.1007/978-981-16-3061-3

This Springer imprint is published by the registered company Springer Nature Singapore Pte Ltd.
The registered company address is: 152 Beach Road, #21-01/04 Gateway East, Singapore 189721,
Singapore

*To Richard Phillips Feynman (May 11, 1918—February 15, 1988),*

*who SURELY was not joking while he talked about the quantum simulator in early eighties.*

# Preface

If you are asking about quantum computation, the easiest way is to search the internet and learn the basics. A series of introductory pieces are available at https://www. nist.gov/history-and-future-quantum-information. On the other hand, if you have a basic idea of the quantum paradigm, as well as high-school level understanding of mathematics and programming, then the first thing you may like to do is to write a program that will run on a quantum computer. There are many such computing facilities available, and the most popular one is possibly the IBM Quantum platform at https://www.ibm.com/quantum-computing/. IBM Quantum provides a nice platform to write programs that run on a quantum computer (naturally with some limitations at this stage). Our first motivation in this book is that a person with knowledge of basic programming and high-school mathematics should be able to connect to the machine and then start writing a program as soon as possible. This is why this book starts with a simple explanation of a quantum computer and immediately dives into writing simple programs. The elementary building blocks of the quantum computing paradigm and how to write programs on such a platform are thus the motivations of the very first chapter.

It is needless to explain that just writing a few programs in Qiskit (the API for using the IBM Quantum platform available at https://qiskit.org) cannot be the only motivation for writing a book in the domain of quantum computing. We want to see our research-minded readers start designing and implementing practical algorithms that are related to Boolean functions. One must be knowing that the first few quantum algorithms that demonstrate superiority over the classical computing paradigm are actually based on Boolean functions. These are the algorithms named after Deutsch, Jozsa, Grover, and Simon. We directly take up the algorithms around Deutsch-Jozsa and explain the program codes on the IBM Quantum platform in the second chapter. The focus is on Boolean functions in this chapter and, in particular, the relationship between the Deutsch-Jozsa algorithm and the Walsh spectrum of a Boolean function.

Boolean functions are very easy to understand (but deep in analysis) and the subject covers a significant amount of material in digital circuits, communication theory, VLSI design, computer science, coding theory, and mathematics. Given that nearly every aspect of modern society is based on the internet, security in digital communication is of prime importance. One necessary tool of such security is cryptology. Boolean functions are considered as one of the basic building blocks in cryptographic system design. The properties that make a Boolean function suitable for a cryptographic system are mostly combinatorial, and in some cases algebraic. We discuss many of these properties, e.g., balancedness, nonlinearity, resiliency, autocorrelation, and propagation characteristics, in this book.

The two most important aspects towards designing any cipher are 'confusion' and 'diffusion'. The Walsh spectrum of a Boolean function is related to 'confusion' and the autocorrelation spectrum is related to 'diffusion'. While we do not get into the cryptologic impacts to a great extent, the basic idea is as follows. If you are using a Boolean function in a cryptographic design, then the maximum absolute values in both the spectra should be minimized. Thus, obtaining these spectra quickly and analyzing them has been a deep area of research for more than a century. It is now evident that in certain cases we have more efficient quantum algorithms than the classical ones for the analysis of Boolean functions.

Following the explanation of Deutsch-Jozsa in the second chapter, we get into further analysis of Walsh spectrum using Grover's algorithm in the third one. The fourth chapter concentrates on the autocorrelation spectrum. In fact, the third and fourth chapters of this book discuss the state-of-the-art research results in this direction. These algorithms and their implementations might be available in different forums, but we explain those here with two specific objectives in mind: to help the beginners write an involved quantum program from scratch and to sail them towards handling more complicated research problems in the context of analyzing cryptographically significant Boolean functions. The book concludes with a clear research direction in this domain with a list of open problems.

Let us underline that this book is not concerned with quantum attacks on classical public key cryptosystems. It is now well known that most of the discrete log and factorization based classical cryptosystems are insecure against quantum adversaries. This is due to the Shor' algorithm (1994) that shows how factorization can be done efficiently using quantum computing. In fact, NIST has taken a serious initiative in standardizing Post Quantum Public Key Cryptosystems recently (visit https://csrc. nist.gov/projects/post-quantum-cryptography for more details).

From an orthogonal point of view, the motivation of this book follows from the quantum attacks on symmetric key cryptosystems where the security (related to the key size) is immediately reduced by a factor of two due to the Grover's algorithm. From this aspect, we present deeper analysis into several specialized quantum algorithms related to the combinatorial and spectral properties of Boolean functions that are directly related to cryptanalysis. That is, this book can be used by the researchers for getting into quantum cryptanalysis of symmetric cryptosystems such as stream and block ciphers.

Before proceeding further, let us highlight the items expected from this book:

- This book is a timely report of the state-of-the-art analytical techniques in the domain of quantum algorithms related to Boolean functions.

- This brief document is a bridge between new research results published in journal articles and a brief contextual literature review in the domain of spectral properties of Boolean functions from a cryptologic viewpoint.
- It presents a snapshot of quantum computing, one of the most emerging topics in the domain of computer science.
- Apart from the state-of-the-art combinatorial techniques, this book considers how the related programs can be actually implemented on a quantum computer. We consider implementing programs written using Qiskit v0.28.0 on the IBM Quantum platform.
- We provide an in-depth study of the existing quantum algorithms related to Boolean functions, as well as our research results, on this topic.
- This book is a presentation of the core concepts on "analyzing cryptographically significant Boolean functions using quantum algorithms" that research students should understand and be aware of in order to make independent contributions.

One must admit that the cover of a book identifies only the author names; yet the outcome is indirectly a joint effort of many people. In this regard, we like to acknowledge our family members, co-researchers, and friends. We could not have prepared this document without their support, particularly during the COVID-19 pandemic.

We acknowledge our parent institutes, Indraprastha Institute of Information Technology, Delhi (IIIT, first two authors); TCG Centres for Research and Education in Science and Technology, Kolkata (TCG CREST, third author); and Indian Statistical Institute, Kolkata (ISI, last author), for providing us un-paralleled academic independence. It is worth mentioning that the Government of India continuously supported our research through various departments and agencies. In particular, all the authors like to acknowledge the project (2016–2021) "Cryptography & Cryptanalysis: How far can we bridge the gap between Classical and Quantum Paradigm", awarded to the last author (Subhamoy Maitra) by the Scientific Research Council of the Department of Atomic Energy (DAE-SRC), the Board of Research in Nuclear Sciences (BRNS).

The first author likes to thank his team members Nakul Aggarwal (currently a graduate student at the University of Alberta), Sagnik Chatterjee (currently a doctoral student at IIIT-Delhi), and Pravek Sharma (currently an undergraduate student at IIIT-Delhi) for their hard efforts that led to winning the second prize in the international IBM Q Awards—"Teach Me quantum" competition organized by IBM and for the discussions during the preparation of some parts of the book. The last author acknowledges the contribution of Dr. Kaushik Chakraborty (presently a post-doctoral fellow at QuTech, Netherlands) and Mr. Chandra Sekhar Mukherjee (currently studying M. Tech. in Computer Science at Indian Statistical Institute) for several discussions that helped us in the preparation of some parts of this manuscript. Special mention must go to Mr. Suman Dutta, presently a research fellow at Indian Statistical Institute, for reading this book very carefully in the final phase. His and the kind efforts of anonymous reviewers helped in improving the editorial as well as the technical quality of this document to a great extent.

Delhi, India/Kolkata, India                                           Tharrmashastha SAPV
November 2020                                                             Debajyoti Bera
                                                                              Arpita Maitra
                                                                           Subhamoy Maitra

# Contents

# About the Authors

**Tharrmashastha SAPV** is currently pursuing his PhD in Computer Science at IIIT Delhi. He did 5-year integrated MSc in Mathematics with first-class honours from ISERC, Visva Bharati, West Bengal. His area of research is quantum algorithms for Boolean functions. He is a regular contributor of Qiskit. His team won the second prize in IBM's Teach Me Quantum competition in 2019. He was rececently selected as a Qiskit Advocate.

**Dr. Debajyoti Bera** received the B.Tech. degree in computer science and engineering with the Indian Institute of Technology, Kanpur, India, in 2002 and the Ph.D. degree in computer science from Boston University, MA, USA, in 2010. Since 2010, he has been an Assistant Professor with the Indraprastha Institute of Information Technology, New Delhi, India. His current research interests include computational complexity theory and quantum computing, application of algorithmic techniques in data mining, network analysis, and information security.

**Dr. Arpita Maitra** works in the domain of Quantum Information since the year 2001. She completed graduation and post-graduation in Physics from Calcutta University and was awarded the PhD degree from Computer Science & Engineering Department at Jadavpur University. Presently she is an Assistant Professor at TCG-CREST, Kolkata. She has authored more than 20 papers in reputed journals and conferences in the broad area of Quantum Secure Communication.

**Prof. Subhamoy Maitra** is a senior professor at Indian Statistical Institute. He has completed his Bachelors in Electronics and Telecommunications Engineering from Jadavpur University, Calcutta. Then he completed his masters in Computer Science and PhD in Computer Science from Indian Statistical Institute, Kolkata. After a brief working experience in the domain of hardware and software engineering he joined Indian Statistical Institute as a faculty in 1997. He has around 200 research papers in various fields of Cryptology and Quantum Information. He has around 6000 citations and has authored several books as well.

# Chapter 1
# Introduction

**Abstract** In this chapter we explain the basic components of the quantum paradigm so that one can start writing programs on a suitable platform. We describe several basic features of quantum bits (qubits) and related operations such as quantum gates, and explain how they operate. We also try to explain how working on a quantum platform provides additional advantages over the classical ones. In this regard, teleportation, super-dense coding and CHSH game are discussed. We support the discussion with codes written in Qiskit SDK

**Keywords** CHSH game · Entanglement · Measurement · No-Cloning · Qubits · Quantum gates · Superposition · Teleportation

## 1.1 Qubit

A Qubit (or quantum bit) is the foundational unit of quantum computation. It can be conceived as the quantum counterpart of the classical bits. A state of some system broadly means the configuration of the system in consideration. To understand this better, consider the following example: Let us think of a 6-faced die. Then the system under consideration is the die and the possible states are '1','2','3','4','5' and '6', which are the possible outcomes we would obtain on rolling a die.

> **Definition 1.1.1: Qubit**
>
> A quantum bit or a qubit is a quantum version of the classical binary bit. A qubit is the basic unit of quantum information.

We can see that a classical bit can only be in one of the two states at any given time usually denoted by 0 and 1. A qubit, in contrast to a classical bit, can be in a *superposition* of multiple states. What does superposition mean? Superposition is the property of a qubit to exist in multiple different states at the same time. In Dirac's

T. SAPV et al., *Quantum Algorithms for Cryptographically Significant Boolean Functions*, SpringerBriefs in Computer Science, https://doi.org/10.1007/978-981-16-3061-3_1

notation where a ket denoted by represents a column vector and a bra denoted by corresponds to a row vector, a single qubit state is represented as

$$|\psi\rangle = \alpha \, |0\rangle + \beta \, |1\rangle \, , \tag{1.1}$$

where $\alpha, \beta \in \mathbb{C}$ are called the amplitudes of $|0\rangle$ and $|1\rangle$ respectively and $\mathbb{C}$ is the set of all complex numbers. $\alpha$ and $\beta$ must satisfy $|\alpha|^2 + |\beta|^2 = 1$—this is called as normalization and is related to sum of probabilities of observing different outcomes being 1. Let us now proceed to explain superposition.

---

**Definition 1.1.2: Superposition**

Superposition is the ability of a quantum system to exist in multiple states at the same time.

---

Any single qubit state can be written as a linear combination of the states $|0\rangle$ and $|1\rangle$. Hence, the states $|0\rangle$ and $|1\rangle$ are called the computational basis states of one qubit. The computational basis of one qubit is generally written as the set $\{|0\rangle, |1\rangle\}$, that is related to measurement of qubits. The exact details on how this is related to measurement will be described in Sect. 1.3. The norm-square of the amplitude of a basis state $|x\rangle$ gives us the probability of obtaining $|x\rangle$ on measuring the qubit. So, on measuring a state of the form in (1.1), we would observe $|0\rangle$ with probability $|\alpha|^2$ and $|1\rangle$ with probability $|\beta|^2$. An immediate question that arises is how a qubit is different from a probabilistic bit. Note that a probabilistic bit $q = (p_0, p_1)$ is a classical bit such that on measuring q we obtain 0 with probability $p_0$ and 1 with probability $p_1$. We will answer this question in the next section.

The state of a qubit can also be represented as a 2-dimensional complex unit vector. The states $|0\rangle$ and $|1\rangle$ represent the vectors

$$|0\rangle \equiv \begin{bmatrix} 1 \\ 0 \end{bmatrix} \qquad\qquad |1\rangle \equiv \begin{bmatrix} 0 \\ 1 \end{bmatrix}. \tag{1.2}$$

Using these representations, we can see that an arbitrary state $|\psi\rangle = \alpha \, |0\rangle + \beta \, |1\rangle$ can be represented as

$$|\psi\rangle = \alpha \, |0\rangle + \beta \, |1\rangle \equiv \alpha \begin{bmatrix} 1 \\ 0 \end{bmatrix} + \beta \begin{bmatrix} 0 \\ 1 \end{bmatrix} = \begin{bmatrix} \alpha \\ \beta \end{bmatrix}. \tag{1.3}$$

The vector notation is a very useful tool to understand the evolution of a state. Many sophisticated quantum computer simulators use the vector notation to simulate the evolution of the qubits of a system.

Now, let us see how we can write a program to initialize a qubit. Initializing a qubit is similar to setting the value of a variable to an integer or floating point number in a programming language. To perform this, we refer to the IBM Quantum platform. As per the IBM Quantum website https://www.ibm.com/quantum-computing/,

"IBM Quantum Services provides a secure, portable, containerized runtime and programming tools to access the latest world-leading cloud-based quantum systems and simulators via the IBM Cloud."

Detailed information regarding this can be found at https://www.ibm.com/quantum-computing/. The programming SDK Qiskit is available at https://qiskit.org/–all the examples in this book are written using Qiskit v0.28.0. As the web pages are quite self-explanatory, we do not detail the installation procedure here and directly get into the programming using the toolkit. In Qiskit, a qubit is initialized in the following manner.

```
1  #Importing the required classes and modules
2  from qiskit import QuantumRegister
3
4  qr = QuantumRegister(1, "q")
```

**Listing 1.1** Qiskit code for initializing a qubit

The above code will initialize a single qubit to $|0\rangle$ and name the qubit as q (naming is optional). Let us break the code to understand better. Line 1 is simply a comment. In line 2, we import the QuantumRegister class which is a necessary step to use the class later. In line 4, we create a QuantumRegister class object and assign it to the variable qr. While instantiating the class, we provide the number of qubits and the name of the qubit as the parameters. Here, we have given the number of qubits as 1 and the name of the qubit as q.

Apart from $|0\rangle$, the state of the qubit qr can also be set to any valid arbitrary state. This is done either by evolving the qubit qr using gates (which we will cover in the next section) or using the initialize() method. For instance, the qubit qr can be set to the quantum state $\frac{1}{\sqrt{2}}|0\rangle + \frac{1}{\sqrt{2}}|1\rangle$ using initialize() as in the following code.

```
1  #Importing the required classes and modules
2  from qiskit import QuantumRegister, QuantumCircuit
3  from math import sqrt
4
5  desired_state = [1/sqrt(2), 1/sqrt(2)]
6  qr = QuantumRegister(1, "q")
7  qc = QuantumCircuit(qr)
8  qc.initialize(desired_state, qr[0])
```

**Listing 1.2** Qiskit code for initializing a qubit to non-zero state

Let us analyze the above code by line. In line 2, we import the QuantumRegister and QuantumCircuit classes. The code in the following line is used to import the "square root" mathematical function. We then assign desired_state the vector $[\alpha, \beta]$, where $\alpha|0\rangle + \beta|1\rangle$ is the state of the qubit we desire to create. Next, we create a QuantumRegister object qr. Line 7 of the code creates a QuantumCircuit object qc with qr as the qubit of the circuit. We then use the initialize() method to initialize the qubit qr to the state specified by desired_state.

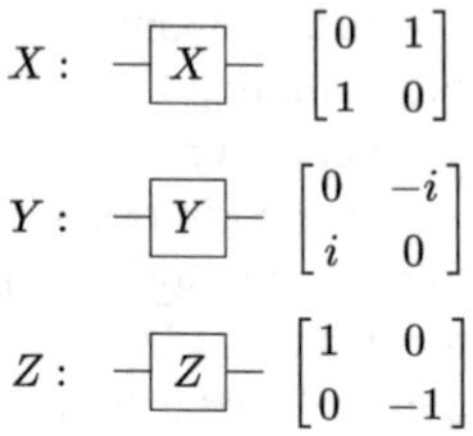

**Fig. 1.1** Common single
qubit gates

$$X : -\boxed{X}- \begin{bmatrix} 0 & 1 \\ 1 & 0 \end{bmatrix}$$

$$Y : -\boxed{Y}- \begin{bmatrix} 0 & -i \\ i & 0 \end{bmatrix}$$

$$Z : -\boxed{Z}- \begin{bmatrix} 1 & 0 \\ 0 & -1 \end{bmatrix}$$

## 1.2 Single Qubit Quantum Gates

Quantum gates are operations that evolve the state of qubit(s). Any gate operation should transform a valid state of a qubit to another valid state of the same. An important characteristic of a quantum gate is that any quantum gate operation is reversible. That is if a quantum gate acts on an input state $|\psi\rangle$ to give some output state $|\phi\rangle$, then given the state $|\phi\rangle$, we should be able to obtain the state $|\psi\rangle$ through some valid quantum gate operation. Vectorially, a gate operation is a transformation from a normalized complex vector to another. These norm preserving operations are performed using unitary transformations. Any unitary transformation can be represented by a unitary matrix. So, corresponding to any quantum gate, there exists a unitary matrix.

> **Definition 1.2.1: Quantum gate**
>
> A quantum gate is an operation that performs a unitary transformation on the state of a qubit. All quantum gates are reversible and can be represented using a unitary matrix.

Let us first consider the single qubit gates. Such gates take a single qubit state as input and produce a single qubit state as output. Three very important and common single qubit quantum gates are the Pauli-X gate, Pauli-Y gate and Pauli-Z gate, also known as the X, Y and Z gates. The matrix representations of these gates are given in Fig. 1.1.

The action of these gates on a qubit $|\psi\rangle = \alpha |0\rangle + \beta |1\rangle$ is given as,

$$X : \begin{bmatrix} 0 & 1 \\ 1 & 0 \end{bmatrix} \begin{bmatrix} \alpha \\ \beta \end{bmatrix} = \begin{bmatrix} \beta \\ \alpha \end{bmatrix}, \qquad Y : \begin{bmatrix} 0 & -i \\ i & 0 \end{bmatrix} \begin{bmatrix} \alpha \\ \beta \end{bmatrix} = \begin{bmatrix} -i\beta \\ i\alpha \end{bmatrix}, \qquad (1.4)$$

$$Z : \begin{bmatrix} 1 & 0 \\ 0 & -1 \end{bmatrix} \begin{bmatrix} \alpha \\ \beta \end{bmatrix} = \begin{bmatrix} \alpha \\ -\beta \end{bmatrix} \qquad (1.5)$$

Using the bra-ket notations, these actions can be described as

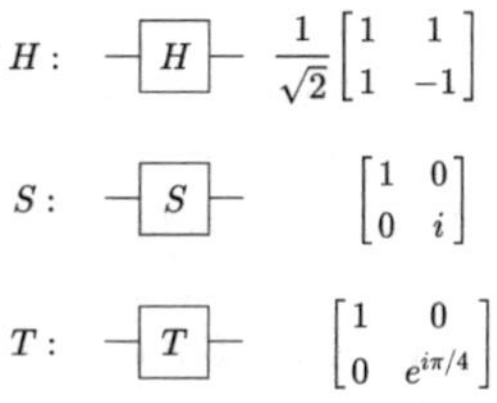

**Fig. 1.2** Matrix
representation of H gate, S
gate and T gate

$$H: \quad -\boxed{H}- \quad \frac{1}{\sqrt{2}}\begin{bmatrix} 1 & 1 \\ 1 & -1 \end{bmatrix}$$

$$S: \quad -\boxed{S}- \quad \begin{bmatrix} 1 & 0 \\ 0 & i \end{bmatrix}$$

$$T: \quad -\boxed{T}- \quad \begin{bmatrix} 1 & 0 \\ 0 & e^{i\pi/4} \end{bmatrix}$$

$$
\begin{aligned}
X\,|\psi\rangle &= X(\alpha\,|0\rangle + \beta\,|1\rangle) \\
&= \alpha X\,|0\rangle + \beta X\,|1\rangle \\
&= \alpha\,|1\rangle + \beta\,|0\rangle
\end{aligned}
\qquad
\begin{aligned}
Y\,|\psi\rangle &= Y(\alpha\,|0\rangle + \beta\,|1\rangle) \\
&= \alpha Y\,|0\rangle + \beta Y\,|1\rangle \\
&= i\alpha\,|1\rangle - i\beta\,|0\rangle
\end{aligned}
$$

$$
\begin{aligned}
Z\,|\psi\rangle &= Z(\alpha\,|0\rangle + \beta\,|1\rangle) \\
&= \alpha Z\,|0\rangle + \beta Z\,|1\rangle \\
&= \alpha\,|0\rangle - \beta\,|1\rangle
\end{aligned}
$$

Note that the X gate acts similar to a classical NOT gate, it flips the state $|0\rangle$ to $|1\rangle$ and vice-versa. The Z gate introduces a relative phase difference of $\pi$ between $|0\rangle$ and $|1\rangle$. In other words, Z gate multiplies a $-1$ to the amplitude of $|1\rangle$. Observe that there does not exist any gate in the classical domain that is analogous to the Z-gate. Decoding the functioning of Y gate is left as an exercise.

A few of the other widely used single qubit gates are the Hadamard gate (or H gate), the S gate and the T gate. The matrix representations of these gates are given in Fig. 1.2.

Now, if H gate is applied on $|0\rangle$, we get $\frac{1}{\sqrt{2}}\begin{pmatrix} 1 & 1 \\ 1 & -1 \end{pmatrix} \cdot \begin{pmatrix} 1 \\ 0 \end{pmatrix} = \frac{1}{\sqrt{2}}\begin{pmatrix} 1 \\ 1 \end{pmatrix}$ which is the vector representation of the state $\frac{1}{\sqrt{2}}(|0\rangle + |1\rangle)$. Similarly, when H is applied on $|1\rangle$, we get $\frac{1}{\sqrt{2}}\begin{pmatrix} 1 \\ -1 \end{pmatrix}$ which corresponds to the state $\frac{1}{\sqrt{2}}(|0\rangle - |1\rangle)$. If we denote $\frac{1}{\sqrt{2}}(|0\rangle + |1\rangle)$ as $|+\rangle$ and $\frac{1}{\sqrt{2}}(|0\rangle - |1\rangle)$ as $|-\rangle$, then we can write as follows.

$$|+\rangle \equiv H\,|0\rangle = \frac{1}{\sqrt{2}}(|0\rangle + |1\rangle), \tag{1.6}$$

$$|-\rangle \equiv H\,|1\rangle = \frac{1}{\sqrt{2}}(|0\rangle - |1\rangle). \tag{1.7}$$

We can see the state $|+\rangle$ as an equal superposition of the states $|0\rangle$ and $|1\rangle$. So, when a unitary is applied on $|+\rangle$, it is essentially being applied on both $|0\rangle$ and $|1\rangle$

simultaneously. This feature of quantum computing where a single operation acts on all states simultaneously in parallel is called quantum parallelism. We will see in the later sections that quantum parallelism helps us to solve several problems in an efficient manner. Notice that the states $\{|+\rangle, |-\rangle\}$ are orthogonal to each other. Similar to the computational basis, these states form another basis. Two states are said to be orthogonal to each other if the dot product of their corresponding vectors is 0. Thus, the set $\{|+\rangle, |-\rangle\}$ also forms a basis for the vector space of one qubit states and this is commonly referred to as the Hadamard basis. Observe that for any qubit in the state $|+\rangle$ or $|-\rangle$, the probability of observing $|0\rangle$ on measurement is $\frac{1}{2}$ and that of $|1\rangle$ is $\frac{1}{2}$ too. Thus, it is not possible to distinguish $|+\rangle$ and $|-\rangle$ by just measuring them in the computational basis.

A quantum circuit is not very different from a classical circuit. It is a collection of qubits, classical bits, operations and wires that defines the flow of the operations on the qubits and the classical bits. However, one should always note that any quantum circuit must be reversible. Let us now see how we implement the gates in Qiskit. The syntax for the above mentioned gates are as follows.

```
1  qc.x(q)    #X gate
2
3  qc.y(q)    #Y gate
4
5  qc.z(q)    #Z gate
6
7  qc.h(q)    #H gate
8
9  qc.s(q)    #S gate
10
11 qc.t(q)    #T gate
```

**Listing 1.3**  Qiskit syntax for a few single qubit gates

Here, qc is a circuit object and q is a single qubit upon which the gate operation is applied. Below we present a code that implements the gates H, Z and X in the same order to obtain the state $\frac{1}{\sqrt{2}}(|1\rangle - |0\rangle)$ from $|0\rangle$.

```
1  #Importing the required classes and modules
2  from qiskit import QuantumRegister, QuantumCircuit
3
4  qr = QuantumRegister(1)
5  qc = QuantumCircuit(qr)
6
7  qc.h(qr)
8  qc.z(qr)
9  qc.x(qr)
10
11 qc.draw()
```

**Listing 1.4**  Qiskit code implementing H, Z and X gates

We will now see how the above code evolves the qubit from the state $|0\rangle$ to the state $\frac{1}{\sqrt{2}}(|1\rangle - |0\rangle)$. The behaviour of the instructions given in lines 1 to 6 are as discussed before. In line 7, the quantum circuit qc starts with Hadamard gate H

**Fig. 1.3** Circuit diagram for the code

which is applied on the qubit qr. The variable qr, by default, was initialized as $|0\rangle$. After the application of H, the state of qr becomes $\frac{1}{\sqrt{2}}(|0\rangle + |1\rangle)$. Line 8 indicates that Z gate is inserted in qc and is applied on qr. So qr now evolves to $\frac{1}{\sqrt{2}}(|0\rangle - |1\rangle)$ (Z changes the phase of $|1\rangle$ by $\pi$). In line 9, X gate is applied on qr. As X behaves similar to a NOT gate, qr finally evolves to $\frac{1}{\sqrt{2}}(|1\rangle - |0\rangle)$. The .draw() method at line 11, prints the quantum circuit corresponding to the operations performed in qc.

Now, we run the code in a Qiskit environment. The execution of the code generates the diagram in Fig. 1.3. Note that in the circuit diagram q_0 represents the qubit qr.

Next, we introduce a generalization of the single qubit gates. A general single qubit gate can be specified by the parametric $U_3$ gate which is defined as

$$U_3(\theta, \phi, \lambda) = \begin{bmatrix} \cos\frac{\theta}{2} & -e^{i\lambda}\sin\frac{\theta}{2} \\ e^{i\phi}\sin\frac{\theta}{2} & e^{i(\phi+\lambda)}\cos\frac{\theta}{2} \end{bmatrix} \tag{1.8}$$

In terms of the $U_3$ gate, the X gate can be expressed as $U_3(\pi, 0, \pi)$; similarly, the H gate can be expressed as $U_3(\frac{\pi}{2}, 0, \pi)$. Two other common parametric gates are $U_1$ and $U_2$ which are defined as

$$U_1(\lambda) = \begin{bmatrix} 1 & 0 \\ 0 & e^{i\lambda} \end{bmatrix} = U_3(0, 0, \lambda) \tag{1.9}$$

$$U_2(\phi, \lambda) = \frac{1}{\sqrt{2}} \begin{bmatrix} 1 & -e^{i\lambda} \\ e^{i\phi} & e^{i(\phi+\lambda)} \end{bmatrix} = U_3(\frac{\pi}{2}, \phi, \lambda) \tag{1.10}$$

The syntax for the $U_1$, $U_2$ and $U_3$ gates in Qiskit are

```
1 qc.u1(lambde, q)  #U1 gate
2
3 qc.u2(phi, lambde, q)  #U2 gate
4
5 qc.u3(theta, phi, lambde, q)  #U3 gate
```
**Listing 1.5** Qiskit syntax for the generic U gates

where theta, phi and lambde are the angles as defined with respect to the gates, qc is the quantum circuit and q is the qubit on which the operation is being applied. We have implemented a code above that produces the state $\frac{1}{\sqrt{2}}(|1\rangle - |0\rangle)$ from $|0\rangle$ using H, Z and X gates. Now we will implement the same circuit but using the $U$ gates. Consider the following code.

```
1  #Importing the required classes and modules
2  from qiskit import QuantumRegister, QuantumCircuit
3  from qiskit import Aer, execute
4  from math import pi
5
6  qr = QuantumRegister(1)
7  qc = QuantumCircuit(qr)
8
9  qc.u2(0, pi, qr)
10 qc.u1(pi, qr)
11 qc.u3(pi, 0, pi, qr)
12
13 #Executing the circuit in a statevector simulator
14 backend = Aer.get_backend('statevector_simulator')
15 qjob = execute(qc,backend)
16 out_vector = qjob.result().get_statevector()
17 print(out_vector)
```

**Listing 1.6**  Qiskit code using the U gates

```
1  Output:
2  [-0.70710678+8.65956056e-17j   0.70710678+0.00000000e
      +00j]
```

The first two line of the code should look familiar now. In line 3, we import Qiskit Aer provided by IBM Quantum Experience. The Qiskit Aer API provides a high performance simulator framework for the Qiskit software stack.[1] In line 4, we import the mathematical constant $\pi$. The following blank line is for beautification. Next, in lines 6 and 7, we define qr as a quantum register object and qc as a quantum circuit object using the qubit qr, respectively. We leave one blank line for decoration. We apply $U_2$ gate on qr by specifying the parameters $\phi = 0$ and $\lambda = \pi$. Then, we apply $U_1$ on qr specifying $\phi = \pi$ in line 10. In line 11, we then apply $U_3$ gate on qr with the parameters $\theta = \pi$, $\phi = 0$ and $\lambda = \pi$. Line 13 is a comment that states that the quantum circuit will be executed in the state vector form. In line 14, the code Aer.get_backend('statevector_simulator') sets the backend as statevector simulator. A backend is the device on which the quantum program is implemented. A statevector simulator is a quantum simulator that simulates the given circuit on a traditional (classical) computer. As the name suggests, the simulation result obtained on using a statevector simulator is a vector that corresponds to the final state of the circuit. Qiskit also provides other simulators like QASM simulator and unitary simulator, and other machines that are truly quantum. The command execute() with the parameters qc and backend used in line 15 executes the circuit qc on backend. Executing a circuit in statevector simulator returns a job object from which we obtain a result object that contains the resultant state of the circuit as a complex vector which is stored as out_vec here. Naming of the result object is at the liberty of the user. One may find that in the following codes, we use different names for result objects. The complex vector itself is obtained from the result object using result().get_statevector(). On executing the code in

---

[1] Visit https://qiskit.org/documentation/apidoc/aer.html for the API documentation of Qiskit Aer.

Qiskit Notebook, we obtain the state $\frac{1}{\sqrt{2}}(|1\rangle - |0\rangle)$ in a form of a complex vector as shown in the output.

In the previous section, we had questioned the difference between a probabilistic bit and a qubit. Note that we work with amplitudes when dealing with qubits, but when we deal with probabilistic bits we turn to probabilities. Then, the natural question that comes to the mind is that if the norm-squares of the amplitudes are probabilities, then why should it be any different from the probabilistic bits? The answer swiftly follows in the next difference that the operations performed on a qubit are unitary operations and hence unitary matrices are used. However, as for probabilistic bits the transition operations are performed using stochastic matrices. Now, the question is what is a stochastic matrix? Stochastic matrices are matrices such that the sum of elements across any row or any column add up to 1. So, the stochastic matrices need not necessarily be unitary matrices. The third prime difference is that during a transformation of a qubit, it is the amplitudes that add or subtract from each other. But in an operation on probabilistic bits, the probabilities get modified. That is how the probabilistic bits are essentially different from the qubits.

## 1.3 Single Qubit Measurement

In the previous sections we got informed about a qubit and operations on the qubit. But a qubit is of no use if we cannot extract information from it. Qubit measurement comes to our aid here. Measurement is the process of observing the state of a qubit. Measurement is also a qubit operation. However, unlike the single qubit gates, measurement is not a unitary operation, and not even reversible. Measuring a qubit gives one bit of information. The peculiarity of measurement is that observing a qubit "collapses", i.e, changes the state of the qubit to one of the basis states.

For instance, if we measure a qubit of the form $\frac{1}{\sqrt{2}}(|0\rangle + |1\rangle)$, we obtain $|0\rangle$ with probability $\frac{1}{2}$ and $|1\rangle$ with probability $\frac{1}{2}$. The $\frac{1}{2}$ is obtained by squaring the absolute value of the amplitude of the respective states. But what does this probability mean?

This can be explained as follows. Consider that someone got access to $n$ number of qubits of the state $\frac{1}{\sqrt{2}}(|0\rangle + |1\rangle)$. Now, suppose he starts measuring each qubit in computational basis. Then, in every instance, he will get either $|0\rangle$ or $|1\rangle$. He never gets $\frac{1}{\sqrt{2}}(|0\rangle + |1\rangle)$ since it is not one of the states of the computational basis—the basis that he measures in. The number of times he observes $|0\rangle$ will almost be equal to the number of times he observes $|1\rangle$. That is of the $n$ measurements, he would observe $|0\rangle$ for about $\frac{n}{2}$ many times and observe $|1\rangle$ for about $\frac{n}{2}$ times. One can say that on measurement, the state of the qubit changes either to the state $|0\rangle$ or into the state $|1\rangle$.

Let us now apply an X gate on a qubit and measure it in Qiskit. The code to perform the same is as follows.

```
#Importing the required classes and modules
from qiskit import QuantumRegister, ClassicalRegister
```

```
 3 from qiskit import QuantumCircuit, Aer, execute
 4
 5 #Creating the quantum register, classical register
 6 #and the quantum circuit
 7 qr = QuantumRegister(1)
 8 cr = ClassicalRegister(1)
 9 qc = QuantumCircuit(qr,cr)
10
11 #Flippling the qubit qr and measuring it
12 qc.x(qr)
13 qc.measure(qr,cr)
14
15 #Executing the circuit in the quantum simulator
16 backend = Aer.get_backend('qasm_simulator')
17 qjob = execute(qc,backend, shots=100)
18 measurement = qjob.result().get_counts()
19 print(measurement)
```

**Listing 1.7**  Qiskit code demonstrating measurement

```
 1 Output:
 2 {'1': 100}
```

For the above code we will discuss the new commands which have not appeared yet. Note that here, apart from the usual class imports, we have also imported the ClassicalRegister class. In line 4 of the code we created an instance `cr` of ClassicalRegister class which helps in storing the output of a qubit measurement. The code `qc.measure(qr,cr)` measures the qubit `qr` and stores the output in `cr`. Here, we set the backend as `qasm_simulator`. In the `execute()` method used here, apart from providing the quantum circuit and the backend as parameters, we have also provided a new parameter `shots`. The `shots` keyword is used to specify the number of times we would want the circuit to be repeated. For instance, in the above code, we have set `shots=100`. So, the circuit (including the measurement) will be executed a total of 100 times and the resulting measurement statistic will be stored in the result object. This operation mimics the fact that someone measures 100 qubits in computational basis.

The default value of `shots` is set as 1024 when it is not explicitly provided as a parameter in the `execute()` method. The QASM simulator simulates the quantum circuit and outputs a result object that contains the measurement outcomes. The measurement results are obtained from the result object using `result().get_counts()`. Note that here, the counts statistic is stored in `measurement`. In our case, X gate is being applied on the qubit `qr`. As the default state of `qr` was $|0\rangle$, the state after application of X gate will be $|1\rangle$. Hence, on measuring the qubit `qr`, we expect to obtain $|1\rangle$ with probability 1. Since we set the number of shots as 100, it is expected that we will obtain the outcome $|1\rangle$ a 100 times. That is exactly what we can observe from the output result.

The measurement we performed in the above example was performed in the computational basis. That is the qubit collapses either to $|0\rangle$ or $|1\rangle$ on measurement. However, if we are interested to know whether the output is $|+\rangle$ or $|-\rangle$, what should we do? In that case, we have to measure the state in the Hadamard basis, i.e, in $\{|+\rangle, |-\rangle\}$ basis. In fact, we can measure the state of a qubit in any arbitrary orthogonal basis according to our need using techniques similar to the one discussed below.

Suppose we have a state $|\phi\rangle = \alpha |0\rangle + \beta |1\rangle$. This state can be written in Hadamard basis as

$$|\phi\rangle = \frac{(\alpha + \beta)}{\sqrt{2}} |+\rangle + \frac{(\alpha - \beta)}{\sqrt{2}} |-\rangle. \tag{1.11}$$

Now on applying $H^\dagger$ on $|\phi\rangle$ we get

$$H^\dagger |\phi\rangle = \frac{(\alpha + \beta)}{\sqrt{2}} |0\rangle + \frac{(\alpha - \beta)}{\sqrt{2}} |1\rangle \tag{1.12}$$

where $H^\dagger$ is the conjugate transpose of H. Observe that $H^\dagger$ maps $|+\rangle$ to $|0\rangle$ and $|-\rangle$ to $|1\rangle$ but while preserving the amplitudes. If we measure $H^\dagger |\phi\rangle$ in computational basis, then it is equivalent to measuring the state $|\phi\rangle$ in the Hadamard basis. Such transformation of bases is universal, i.e, if we have an access to a device that can measure only in computational basis then by applying a transformation (here, $H^\dagger$), we can transform the computational basis to the basis of our interest. We will now employ this technique while implementing a measurement in Hadamard basis in Qiskit.

The following code applies an X gate on the qubit and measures the qubit in Hadamard basis.

```
#Importing the required classes and modules
from qiskit import QuantumRegister, ClassicalRegister
from qiskit import QuantumCircuit, Aer, execute

#Creating the quantum register, classical register
#and the quantum circuit
qr = QuantumRegister(1)
cr = ClassicalRegister(1)
qc = QuantumCircuit(qr,cr)

qc.x(qr)

#Mapping Hadamard basis into computational
#basis by applying H^{dag} = H on qr.
qc.h(qr)
qc.measure(qr,cr)

#Executing the circuit in the simulator
backend = Aer.get_backend('qasm_simulator')
qjob = execute(qc,backend)
counts = qjob.result().get_counts()
print(counts)
```

**Listing 1.8** Qiskit code demonstrating measurement in Hadamard basis

**Fig. 1.4** Circuit for a
quantum true random
number generator

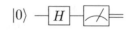

```
1 Output:
2 {'1':  489, '0': 535}
```

Note that for converting the measurement basis from computational basis to Hadamard basis, we apply the H gate on `qr` (line 15). However, we mentioned that we have to apply $H^\dagger$ for the same. Here, one should remember that in case of Hadamard matrix, $H = H^\dagger$. Since we have not mentioned the number of shots, the number of shots is set to to the default value of 1024. The measurement statistic is stored in the variable named `counts` in this code.

From the output, we find that $|0\rangle$ is obtained as the measurement outcome in 489 cases whereas $|1\rangle$ is obtained in 535 cases out of a total of 1024 cases. So, the probability of getting $|0\rangle$ is $489/1024 = 0.477$ and the probability of getting $|1\rangle$ is $535/1024 = 0.522$. Theoretically, the probabilities should be equal, however, due to the randomness in the measurement we observe the deviation away from $\frac{1}{2}$. Remember that here the outcome $|0\rangle$ corresponds to the state $|+\rangle$ and the outcome $|1\rangle$ corresponds to the state $|-\rangle$.

### Quantum True Random Number Generators (QTRNG)

In this subsection we will discuss a very simple, however very important application of a single qubit gate—Hadamard gate. We will show how Hadamard gate and measurement in computational basis provide us true random sequences.

Random number generators are the heart of many fields, specially cryptography. However, as the classical computers are deterministic, obtaining true randomness from those is not possible. Most of the applications of random number generators use the pseudo random number generators whose output 'appears' as random, i.e., looking at the output bit-stream it is computationally or information theoretically hard to distinguish that from true random sequence. However, the same seed generates the same output stream in a deterministic classical computer and hence this is not actually random.

Interestingly, in a quantum setting, it is possible to obtain a true random number generator. We now learnt that on applying Hadamard gate on the state $|0\rangle$, we can obtain the state $\frac{1}{\sqrt{2}}(|0\rangle + |1\rangle)$. The resultant state is such that on measuring it, we get the outcome $|0\rangle$ with probability $\frac{1}{2}$ and $|1\rangle$ with probability $\frac{1}{2}$. In other words, we obtain an output that is truly random in nature. Remember that this true randomness is an inherent property of the quantum states.

The quantum true random number generator can be implemented in Qiskit using the following code:

```
1 #Importing the required classes and modules.
2 from qiskit import QuantumRegister, ClassicalRegister
3 from qiskit import QuantumCircuit, Aer, execute
4
```

```
5  for i in range(10):
6      #Creating quatum register, classical register
7      #and quantum circuit objects.
8      q = QuantumRegister(1)
9      c = ClassicalRegister(1)
10     qc = QuantumCircuit(q,c)
11
12     #Applying the Hadamard gate and measuring the
13     #resultant state
14     qc.h(q)
15     qc.measure(q,c)
16
17     #Executing the circuit in a simulator
18     backend = Aer.get_backend('qasm_simulator')
19     qjob = execute(qc,backend, shots=1)
20     counts = qjob.result().get_counts()
21     for key in counts.keys():
22         print(key)
```

**Listing 1.9** Implementing quantum true random number generator

```
1  Output:
2  1
3  0
4  1
5  0
6  0
7  1
8  0
9  1
10 1
11 1
```

Note that here, we use a "for" loop and set the number of shots as 1. This means that inside each loop the circuit will run only once. The output will be stored in the classical register c. In the output, we obtained 10 key bits as the "for" loop has been executed for 10 times. Every execution of this code might produce different outputs.

Until now we have dealt with single qubits, operations on them and their measurements. It is now time to look beyond single qubit systems and get into multiple qubit systems.

## 1.4 Multiple Qubits

Even though single qubits are instrumental in understanding the bedrock of quantum computing, if we want to actually solve problems of considerable scale, we cannot aim to do that without multiple qubits. A multi-qubit system can be thought of as an extension to the single qubit system. Let us first take a simple scenario of two qubits. If we have two classical bits, then all possible states of the two bit system are 00, 01, 10 and 11. In a quantum setting, similar to a single qubit, a two qubit system can be in a superposition of all four possible states. In Dirac's notation, the two qubit system can be written as

$$|\psi\rangle = \alpha_0 |00\rangle + \alpha_1 |01\rangle + \alpha_2 |10\rangle + \alpha_3 |11\rangle \qquad (1.13)$$

such that $\sum_i |\alpha_i|^2 = 1$ where $\alpha_i \in \mathbb{C}$ for $i \in \{0, 1, 2, 3\}$ are the amplitudes. Here, $|ab\rangle$ is shorthand notation of the tensor product $|a\rangle \otimes |b\rangle$, i.e, $|00\rangle$ means $|0\rangle \otimes |0\rangle$, $|01\rangle$ implies $|0\rangle \otimes |1\rangle$ and so on. Before we proceed further, let us first understand what tensor products are. A tensor product is a mapping defined from a pair of vector spaces to a vector space. Vectorially, for two vectors $|a\rangle = \begin{bmatrix} a_1 \\ \vdots \\ a_n \end{bmatrix}$ and $|b\rangle = \begin{bmatrix} b_1 \\ \vdots \\ b_m \end{bmatrix}$, the tensor product $|a\rangle \otimes |b\rangle$ is given as the vector

$$|a\rangle \otimes |b\rangle = \begin{bmatrix} a_1 \cdot b_1 \\ \vdots \\ a_1 \cdot b_m \\ \vdots \\ a_n \cdot b_1 \\ \vdots \\ a_n \cdot b_m \end{bmatrix}$$

Notice that the tensor product is non-commutative, i.e., $|a\rangle \otimes |b\rangle$ is not necessarily equal to $|b\rangle \otimes |a\rangle$. Also observe that while the dimensions of $|a\rangle$ is $n \times 1$ and that of $|b\rangle$ is $m \times 1$, the dimensions of the tensor product $|a\rangle \otimes |b\rangle$ is $(n \cdot m) \times 1$. Given two single qubits of the form $|c\rangle$ and $|d\rangle$, the tensor product $|c\rangle \otimes |d\rangle$ provides the combined state of the two qubits.

More generally, tensor products are defined on matrices. The fact that vectors are 1-dimensional matrices, lead us to the above definition of tensor product on vectors.

---

**Definition 1.4.1: Tensor product of matrices**

Given two matrices $A = (a_{ij})_{m \times n}$ and $B = (b_{ij})_{p \times q}$ where $a_{ij}, b_{ij} \in \mathbb{C}$, the tensor product of $A$ and $B$ is given as follows:

$$A \otimes B = \begin{pmatrix} a_{11}B & a_{12}B & \cdots & a_{1n}B \\ a_{21}B & a_{22}B & \cdots & a_{2n}B \\ \vdots & & \ddots & \vdots \\ a_{m1}B & a_{m2}B & \cdots & a_{mn}B \end{pmatrix}_{mp \times nq}$$

---

Notice that if the dimensions of a matrix $A$ are $m \times n$ and that of a matrix $B$ are $p \times q$, then the dimensions of the matrix obtained as a result of the tensor product between $A$ and $B$, i.e, $A \otimes B$ will be $mp \times nq$. Let us try to understand this better using an example. We will compute the tensor product of the matrices corresponding to the $X$ gate and the $H$ gate. The tensor product looks as follows:

$$X \otimes H = \begin{bmatrix} 0 & 1 \\ 1 & 0 \end{bmatrix} \otimes \frac{1}{\sqrt{2}} \begin{bmatrix} 1 & 1 \\ 1 & -1 \end{bmatrix} = \frac{1}{\sqrt{2}} \begin{bmatrix} 0 \cdot \begin{bmatrix} 1 & 1 \\ 1 & -1 \end{bmatrix} & 1 \cdot \begin{bmatrix} 1 & 1 \\ 1 & -1 \end{bmatrix} \\ 1 \cdot \begin{bmatrix} 1 & 1 \\ 1 & -1 \end{bmatrix} & 0 \cdot \begin{bmatrix} 1 & 1 \\ 1 & -1 \end{bmatrix} \end{bmatrix} = \frac{1}{\sqrt{2}} \begin{bmatrix} 0 & 0 & 1 & 1 \\ 0 & 0 & 1 & -1 \\ 1 & 1 & 0 & 0 \\ 1 & -1 & 0 & 0 \end{bmatrix}$$

Similar to the tensor product of two vectors, tensor products of matrices are not necessarily commutative. As for the notations, throughout this book, we will use $A \otimes B$ to denote the tensor product of the matrix $A$ with $B$ and the notation $A \cdot B$ or $AB$ will be used to denote the matrix product of $A$ with $B$.

A column vector containing the amplitude of $|\psi\rangle$ is used as the notation for a state $|\psi\rangle$, i.e,

$$|\psi\rangle = \begin{bmatrix} \alpha_0 \\ \alpha_1 \\ \alpha_2 \\ \alpha_3 \end{bmatrix}. \tag{1.14}$$

A system composed of two qubits of state, say $|\phi_1\rangle$ and $|\phi_2\rangle$, can be written as

$$|\psi\rangle = |\phi_1\rangle \otimes |\phi_2\rangle. \tag{1.15}$$

Similarly, the state of an $n$-qubit system that constitutes of $n$ single qubits, with states say $|\phi_1\rangle \cdots |\phi_n\rangle$, can be written as

$$|\psi\rangle = |\phi_1\rangle \otimes |\phi_2\rangle \otimes \cdots \otimes |\phi_n\rangle. \tag{1.16}$$

Using the individual states of each of the qubits, Eq. 1.16 provides us a way to represent the complete $n$ qubit system. However, given an arbitrary $n$ qubit quantum system is it always possible to express that as a tensor product of $n$ single qubit states? This is not necessarily true. To understand why, we first introduce another fundamental property of qubits called *entanglement*.

**Quantum Entanglement**

Entanglement is another property of qubits that differentiate them from the classical bits. Consider the following two qubit state

$$|\psi\rangle = \frac{1}{\sqrt{2}}(|00\rangle + |11\rangle). \tag{1.17}$$

The state $|\psi\rangle$ above cannot be written as a tensor product of two single qubit states. The state of any one of the two qubits alone cannot be determined in a precise manner. In this case, the two qubits are said to be in an entanglement. Extending the definition to arbitrary number of qubits, if the state of a system of $n$ qubits cannot be written as a tensor product of two independent states, then the qubits in the system are said to be in an entanglement with each other.

---

**Definition 1.4.2: Entanglement**

A set of qubits whose combined state is $|\psi\rangle$ is said to be in a state of entanglement if $|\psi\rangle$ cannot be decomposed as $|\psi\rangle = |\phi\rangle \otimes |\xi\rangle$ where $|\phi\rangle$ and $|\xi\rangle$ are two independent quantum states.

---

Let us now look at an interesting property of entanglement. Consider the state defined in (1.17). We can observe that on measuring the first qubit, we would obtain $|0\rangle$ with probability $\frac{1}{2}$ and $|1\rangle$ with probability $\frac{1}{2}$. The same is the situation if we measure the second qubit first. Now, let us assume that we have measured the first qubit and obtained $|0\rangle$. Then, on measuring the second qubit, with probability 1 we will observe $|0\rangle$ because of the fact that the measurement on the first qubit has collapsed the state of the system to $|00\rangle$. Similarly if our measurement outcome is $|1\rangle$ after measuring the first qubit, then with certainty we would obtain $|1\rangle$ for second qubit. So from just measuring any one of the qubits, we can learn about the measurement outcome for the remaining qubit. An important point to note is that the outcome of the first measurement is probabilistic, i.e, the outcomes $|0\rangle$ or $|1\rangle$ will occur with equal probability. However, once the measurement has done, the state of the remaining qubit will be determined exactly.

Some of the most important two-qubit states are the Bell states. Those states are also familiarly known as EPR pairs (the name EPR comes from the name of the scientists Einstein, Podolsky and Rosen). The states are given as follows.

$$|\Phi^+\rangle = \frac{1}{\sqrt{2}}(|00\rangle + |11\rangle)$$

$$|\Phi^-\rangle = \frac{1}{\sqrt{2}}(|00\rangle - |11\rangle)$$

$$|\Psi^+\rangle = \frac{1}{\sqrt{2}}(|01\rangle + |10\rangle)$$

$$|\Psi^-\rangle = \frac{1}{\sqrt{2}}(|01\rangle - |10\rangle).$$

Bell states are very widely used in quantum computation. It is the fundamental component in quantum teleportation and super dense coding which we will discuss in later sections. It is also used in algorithms in quantum cryptography for secure communications.

Very similar to the Bell states, there are three qubit entangled state known as the GHZ states (Greenberger-Horne-Zeilinger states). The states are written as

$$|GHZ_\pm\rangle = \frac{1}{\sqrt{2}}(|000\rangle \pm |111\rangle). \tag{1.18}$$

The GHZ states are extensively used in quantum error correction, which we will not be able to discuss in this book.

## 1.5 Multi-Qubit Gates

Consider a system of two qubits. We want to perform a NOT operation on the second qubit only if the state of the first qubit is $|1\rangle$. To achieve this in a classical setting, we just perform an xor of the first and the second bits and store it in the second bit. It is obvious that we cannot perform this operation using single qubit gates because the single qubit gates can only manipulate a single qubit and is independent of the other qubits. So, we need a gate that can interact with two qubits at the same time, in other words, a two qubit gate. To perform the controlled operation mentioned above, we use a CNOT gate, also called a "Controlled-NOT" gate. The CNOT gate has two inputs, a 'control' qubit and a 'target' qubit. If the control qubit is set to $|1\rangle$ then it flips the target qubit and does nothing otherwise. The matrix representation of the CNOT gate is given by the following 4×4 unitary matrix

$$\text{CNOT} := \begin{bmatrix} 1 & 0 & 0 & 0 \\ 0 & 1 & 0 & 0 \\ 0 & 0 & 0 & 1 \\ 0 & 0 & 1 & 0 \end{bmatrix}$$

The action of CNOT on a two qubit state of the form $|\psi\rangle = \alpha_0 |00\rangle + \alpha_1 |01\rangle + \alpha_2 |10\rangle + \alpha_3 |11\rangle$ can be given as

$$CNOT |\psi\rangle = \alpha_0 |00\rangle + \alpha_1 |01\rangle + \alpha_2 |11\rangle + \alpha_3 |10\rangle.$$

Note that while the amplitudes of the states $|00\rangle$ and $|01\rangle$ remained the same as that in the state $|\psi\rangle$, the amplitudes of $|10\rangle$ and $|11\rangle$ have interchanged. A useful way of representing the action of CNOT gate in the ket notation is specifying its action on the computation basis states of the individual qubits.

$$CNOT |a\rangle |b\rangle \longrightarrow |a\rangle |a \oplus b\rangle.$$

One can also think of CNOT as a function that acts on two qubits. In that case, CNOT can be defined as the following function:

$$CNOT(|a\rangle, |b\rangle) \longrightarrow (|a\rangle, |a \oplus b\rangle).$$

CNOT gate is one of the most widely used quantum gates. This is by virtue of the fact that CNOT gate is the most basic quantum gate that allows for interaction between two qubits in a quantum circuit. In fact, any quantum gate can be constructed using the combinations of CNOT gates and the set of all single qubit gates, earning them the title of *universal* quantum gates.

Similar to the CNOT gate, which essentially implements X gate on the target qubit conditioned on the control qubit being $|1\rangle$, we can have other controlled unitary gates. These controlled unitary gates are implemented such that the unitary gate is implemented on the target qubit conditioned on the control qubit being $|1\rangle$. For instance, controlled-Hadamard, denoted $C_H$, is a two qubit controlled unitary gate whose matrix representation is given by the matrix

$$C_H := \begin{bmatrix} 1 & 0 & 0 & 0 \\ 0 & 1 & 0 & 0 \\ 0 & 0 & \frac{1}{\sqrt{2}} & \frac{1}{\sqrt{2}} \\ 0 & 0 & \frac{1}{\sqrt{2}} & -\frac{1}{\sqrt{2}} \end{bmatrix}.$$

An extension of the two qubit CNOT gate is the three qubits Toffoli gate, also called the CCNOT gate. A CCNOT gate takes three inputs; the first two are the control qubits whereas the third qubit is the target qubit. The action of CCNOT on its inputs is such that the target qubit is flipped if and only if both the control qubits are set to 1. More formally, the action of CCNOT gate on the set of inputs $|a\rangle |b\rangle |c\rangle$ is expressed as

$$CCNOT \, |a\rangle \, |b\rangle \, |c\rangle \longrightarrow |a\rangle \, |b\rangle \, |c \oplus (a \cdot b)\rangle$$

where $(\cdot)$ represents the bitwise *AND* operation. Since, CCNOT gate operates on three qubits, its corresponding unitary matrix is of dimensions $8 \times 8$ and is as given below.

$$CCNOT := \begin{bmatrix} 1 & 0 & 0 & 0 & 0 & 0 & 0 & 0 \\ 0 & 1 & 0 & 0 & 0 & 0 & 0 & 0 \\ 0 & 0 & 1 & 0 & 0 & 0 & 0 & 0 \\ 0 & 0 & 0 & 1 & 0 & 0 & 0 & 0 \\ 0 & 0 & 0 & 0 & 1 & 0 & 0 & 0 \\ 0 & 0 & 0 & 0 & 0 & 1 & 0 & 0 \\ 0 & 0 & 0 & 0 & 0 & 0 & 0 & 1 \\ 0 & 0 & 0 & 0 & 0 & 0 & 1 & 0 \end{bmatrix}$$

The CNOT gates and CCNOT gates are available in Qiskit. The syntax for applying a CNOT in a quantum circuit qc is illustrated in this example (Listing 1.10).

```
#CNOT Gate with q0 as control qubit
#and q2 as the target qubit
qc.cx(q0, q2)
```

**Listing 1.10** Qiskit code for implementing CNOT gate

Here, q0 is the control qubit and q2 is the target qubit. Similarly the syntax for implementation of CCNOT in qc is illustrated in Listing 1.11 where q0 and q1 are the control qubits and q2 is the target qubit. Note that, here, q0, q1 or q2 are the variables that contain the QuantumRegister instance.

```
1  #CCNOT Gate with q0 and q1 as control qubits
2  #and q2 as the target qubit
3  qc.ccx(q0, q1, q2)
```

**Listing 1.11** Qiskit code for implementing Toffoli gate

We will now see some interesting applications of these multi-qubit gates, specifically the two-qubit CNOT gate. One wonderful application of CNOT gate is as a quantum cloning machine for states in computational basis. Generally, in quantum domain cloning an unknown, arbitrary state is not possible.

**No Cloning Theorem**

We earlier saw that measuring a qubit of the form $|\psi\rangle = \alpha |0\rangle + \beta |1\rangle$ collapses the qubit to either $|0\rangle$ or $|1\rangle$. Once the qubit collapses, the information about $\alpha$ and $\beta$ are lost forever. If we are provided with a qubit of the form $|\psi\rangle$ where the amplitudes are unknown, is it possible to obtain $\alpha$ and $\beta$? If we are given a lot of qubits, all in the same state $|\psi\rangle$, then we can measure each qubit and get an estimate of $\alpha$ and $\beta$. But what if we are provided with just a single qubit in the state $|\psi\rangle$? We could apply the same strategy if we know how to make multiple copies of $|\psi\rangle$, also known as cloning. So, we need a circuit that takes the state $|\psi\rangle$ and an ancilla as inputs and outputs two copies of $|\psi\rangle$. Ancilla, short for ancillary qubits, are additional qubits initialized to some fixed state, usually $|0\rangle$; they play the role of variables used in programs for storing the output values or intermediate values.

Let us explore the possibility of existence of such a circuit. For states in the computational basis, CNOT serves the purpose. When the CNOT gate is provided with $|0\rangle |0\rangle$ as input, we get

$$CNOT \, |0\rangle |0\rangle \longrightarrow |0\rangle |0\rangle .$$

Similarly, if we provide $|1\rangle |0\rangle$ as input, we get

$$CNOT \, |1\rangle |0\rangle \longrightarrow |1\rangle |1\rangle .$$

So, the CNOT looks like a plausible candidate for the copying circuit. However, is it true for all the single qubit state? That is, given any single qubit and an ancilla in state $|0\rangle$, will CNOT copy the state on the ancilla? Let's test it out.

Suppose the single qubit state is denoted $|\psi\rangle$. We observe the following:

$$CNOT (\alpha |0\rangle + \beta |1\rangle) |0\rangle \longrightarrow \alpha |0\rangle |0\rangle + \beta |1\rangle |1\rangle$$

We end up in an entanglement! What we wanted was the state

$$|\psi\rangle \otimes |\psi\rangle = (\alpha\,|0\rangle + \beta\,|1\rangle) \otimes (\alpha\,|0\rangle + \beta\,|1\rangle)$$

which can be easily verified to be different from the state we obtain. So, CNOT gate cannot be the copying circuit for arbitrary qubits. In fact, we cannot have *any circuit* that makes copies of an arbitrary state without fail. This property of "the non-existence of a copying circuit" is called the *no-cloning* theorem. The formal statement of the no-cloning theorem is given in Theorem 1.1.

**Theorem 1.1** *There does not exist any unitary U such that given any unknown arbitrary input state* $|\psi\rangle$ *and a fixed state, U performs the following operation.*

$$U\,|\psi\rangle\,|j\rangle \longrightarrow |\psi\rangle\,|\psi\rangle$$

***Proof*** Let $|\psi\rangle$ and $|\phi\rangle$ be two arbitrary, distinct states and let us assume that there exists a universal $U$ that acts as

$$U\,|\psi\rangle\,|j\rangle \longrightarrow |\psi\rangle\,|\psi\rangle\,, \qquad U\,|\phi\rangle\,|j\rangle \longrightarrow |\phi\rangle\,|\phi\rangle\,.$$

Then using the bra-ket notation and the fact that unitary operations preserve the inner product of the state, we have

$$\langle j|\,\langle\psi|\,U^\dagger U\,|\phi\rangle\,|j\rangle = \langle\psi|\,\langle\psi|\,|\phi\rangle\,|\phi\rangle$$
$$\langle\psi|\,|\phi\rangle\,\langle j|\,j\rangle = \langle\psi|\,\phi\rangle\,\langle\psi|\,\phi\rangle \quad (\because U^\dagger U = I \text{ since } U \text{ is unitary})$$
$$\langle\psi|\,\phi\rangle = \langle\psi|\,\phi\rangle^2 \quad (|j\rangle \text{ is normalized})$$

Now, this is possible only if either $|\langle\psi|\,\phi\rangle| = 1$ (i.e., $|\psi\rangle = e^{i\theta}\,|\phi\rangle$ for some $\theta$) or $|\langle\psi|\,\phi\rangle| = 0$ (i.e., $|\psi\rangle$ and $|\phi\rangle$ are orthogonal), but not for any arbitrary state $|\psi\rangle$. This proves the theorem.

**Creating an Entanglement**

During the search for a copying circuit, we ended up with an entangled state when we used a CNOT on the state $(\alpha\,|0\rangle + \beta\,|1\rangle)\,|0\rangle$. Now, we modify our circuit a bit. Instead of only a CNOT gate, we insert another unitary gate, denoted U, that transforms $|0\rangle$ to $\alpha\,|0\rangle + \beta\,|1\rangle$ (we assume that $\alpha$ and $\beta$ are non-zero). Then, the following circuit (Fig. 1.5) provides us a two qubit entangled state of the form $\alpha\,|00\rangle + \beta\,|11\rangle$ where $\alpha \neq 0$ and $\beta \neq 0$. So, from two un-entangled $|0\rangle$ states, we are able to create a two-qubit entangled state.

**Fig. 1.5** Circuit for
entanglement

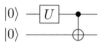

The evolution of the state is given below.

$$|0\rangle\,|0\rangle \xrightarrow{U\otimes I} \Big(\alpha\,|0\rangle + \beta\,|1\rangle\Big)\,|0\rangle \xrightarrow{CNOT} \alpha\,|0\rangle\,|0\rangle + \beta\,|1\rangle\,|1\rangle\,.$$

If U is a Hadamard gate, then what will happen? We will get one of the Bell states:
$|\phi^+\rangle = \frac{1}{\sqrt{2}}(|00\rangle + |11\rangle)$. The Qiskit code for creating the Bell state $|\phi^+\rangle$ is as follows.

```
1  #Importing the classes and modules
2  from qiskit import *
3
4  #Creating quantum register and quantum circuit objects
5  q = QuantumRegister(2)
6  c = ClassicalRegister(2)
7  qc = QuantumCircuit(q,c)
8
9  #Applying the entangling operations
10 qc.h(q[0])
11 qc.cx(q[0],q[1])
12 qc.measure(q,c)
13
14 #Executing the circuit in the simulator
15 backend = Aer.get_backend('qasm_simulator')
16 qjob = execute(qc,backend)
17 counts = qjob.result().get_counts()
18 print(counts)
```

**Listing 1.12** Creating an entanglement

```
1  Output:
2  {'11': 497, '00': 527}
```

Note that, in line 2, we use the command "from qiskit import *". This
implies that all the necessary objects that are embedded in Qiskit will be imported.
Here, we can see that we are considering a quantum register with two qubits and a classical register with two bits using the initializations q = QuantumRegister(2)
and c = ClassicalRegister(2). This is because we are now dealing with
two qubits. The two qubits are placed in an array. First qubit is denoted by q[0]
whereas the second qubit is denoted by q[1]. As for the creation of the entanglement, in the quantum circuit qc, the Hadamard gate (h) is applied on q[0] (line
10) followed by CNOT with q[0] as the control and q[1] as the target qubits,
respectively(line 11). The evolution of the states take place as follows.

$$|0\rangle\,|0\rangle \xrightarrow{H\otimes I} \frac{1}{\sqrt{2}}\Big(|0\rangle + |1\rangle\Big)\,|0\rangle \xrightarrow{CNOT_{0,1}} \frac{1}{\sqrt{2}}\Big(|0\rangle\,|0\rangle + |1\rangle\,|1\rangle\Big).$$

On executing the code, we see from the output that a measurement results either in $|00\rangle$ or in $|11\rangle$, both with equal probability of $\left(\frac{1}{\sqrt{(2)}}\right)^2 = \frac{1}{\sqrt{(2)}}$.

A three qubit *GHZ* state of the form $\frac{1}{\sqrt{2}}(|000\rangle + |111\rangle)$ can be easily obtained using a similar construction. We leave it as an exercise to the reader to construct a circuit for the same.

## 1.6   Multi-Qubit Measurement

In Sect. 1.3, we saw that single qubit measurements are essentially operators but not necessarily unitary. In this section we extend the concept of measurement to more than one qubits. One of the postulates of quantum mechanics describes measurement by a set of operators $\{M_i\}$. These operators are called the measurement operators with measurement outcomes $i$. In terms of vector algebra, a measurement operator $M_i$ can be thought of as a matrix. For a system in state $|\psi\rangle$, the probability of obtaining the outcome $i$ is given by the relation

$$Pr(i) = \langle\psi|M_i^\dagger M_i|\psi\rangle \qquad (1.19)$$

and on obtaining an outcome $i$, the state of the system collapses to

$$|\psi'\rangle = \frac{M_i|\psi\rangle}{\sqrt{\langle\psi|M_i^\dagger M_i|\psi\rangle}}. \qquad (1.20)$$

Observe that the post measurement state is normalized. Let us have a two qubit system of the form $|\psi\rangle = \frac{1}{2}(|00\rangle + |01\rangle + |10\rangle + |11\rangle)$. It is obvious that $|\psi\rangle$ can also be written as $|\psi\rangle = \frac{1}{\sqrt{2}}(|0\rangle + |1\rangle) \otimes \frac{1}{\sqrt{2}}(|0\rangle + |1\rangle)$. Now, define a measurement using the operators $|00\rangle\langle00|$, $|01\rangle\langle01|$, $|10\rangle\langle10|$ and $|11\rangle\langle11|$ associated with the measurement outcomes 00, 01, 10 and 11 respectively. Let the set containing only these operators be $C_M$. This measurement is actually the measurement in the computational basis. Now, the probability of obtaining the outcome 00 upon measuring using $C_M$ is given as

$$Pr(00) = \langle\psi|\,(|00\rangle\langle00|)^\dagger(|00\rangle\langle00|)\,|\psi\rangle. \qquad (1.21)$$

> **Definition 1.6.1: Measurement**
>
> Measurement is the process of observing the state of a qubit to extract information about the qubit. Mathematically, a measurement is described by a set of measurement operators $\{M_i\}$ and each $M_i$ is associated with an outcome $i$. For a system in the state $|\psi\rangle$ just before measurement, the probability of obtaining the outcome $i$ on measuring $|\psi\rangle$ is given by
>
> $$Pr(i) = \langle\psi| M_i^\dagger M_i |\psi\rangle$$
>
> and upon measurement the state $|\psi\rangle$ collapses to
>
> $$|\psi'\rangle = \frac{M_i |\psi\rangle}{\sqrt{\langle\psi| M_i^\dagger M_i |\psi\rangle}}$$
>
> when the outcome $i$ is obtained.

Before we proceed further to compute the probability using the expression 1.21, let us first clear certain grounds. In algebra, $\langle a|$ is the dual of $|a\rangle$. They are related as $\langle a| = (|a\rangle)^\dagger$, i.e, $\langle a|$ is the conjugate transpose of $|a\rangle$. We saw in the previous section that a ket $|a\rangle$ can be represented equivalently as a column vector. Naturally, a bra $\langle a|$ can be represented as a row vector since it is a conjugate transpose of a column vector. The inner product of two kets $|a\rangle$ and $|b\rangle$ is defined as

$$\langle a| b\rangle = (|a\rangle)^\dagger (|b\rangle).$$

In terms of vectors, an inner product of two kets can be perceived as the dot product of the vectors corresponding to the kets. An interesting and useful property of inner product is that the inner product between two vectors $|a\rangle$ and $|b\rangle$ is 0 if they are orthogonal and 1 if they are the identical. An outer product of $|a\rangle$ with $|b\rangle$ is given as $|a\rangle \langle b|$. In terms of vectors, an outer product can be perceived as the product of a column vector with a row vector, yielding a matrix. We can see that that the outer product $|a\rangle \langle b|$ is the same as $(|b\rangle \langle a|)^\dagger$.

Now, going back to the probability of obtaining the outcome 00 on measurement, we had

$$Pr(00) = \langle\psi| (|00\rangle \langle00|)^\dagger (|00\rangle \langle00|) |\psi\rangle .$$

Observe that the product $(|00\rangle \langle00|) |\psi\rangle$ can be evaluated as

$$(|00\rangle \langle 00|) \, |\psi\rangle = |00\rangle \langle 00| \left[ \frac{1}{2}(|00\rangle + |01\rangle + |10\rangle + |11\rangle) \right]$$

$$= \frac{1}{2} |00\rangle \Big( \langle 00| \, 00\rangle + \langle 00| \, 01\rangle + \langle 00| \, 10\rangle + \langle 00| \, 11\rangle \Big)$$

$$= \frac{1}{2} |00\rangle .$$

Note that $\langle \psi| \, (|00\rangle \langle 00|)^{\dagger} = \Big( (|00\rangle \langle 00|) \, |\psi\rangle \Big)^{\dagger}$. Hence we have

$$Pr(00) = (\frac{1}{2} \langle 00|)(\frac{1}{2} |00\rangle) = \frac{1}{4} \langle 00| \, 00\rangle = \frac{1}{4}.$$

The probabilities of obtaining the other measurements can be obtained in a similar manner. In a scenario where we measure just the first qubit of the state $|\psi\rangle$, the probability of obtaining the outcome 0 can be computed as $\frac{1}{2}$. The post measurement state of the system on measuring the first qubit as 0 can be given using Eq. 1.20 as

$$|\psi_0\rangle = \frac{1}{\sqrt{2}}(|00\rangle + |01\rangle).$$

An important property in measurement is that the set of measurement operators satisfy the following relation

$$\sum_i M_i^{\dagger} M_i = I. \tag{1.22}$$

This relation is known as the completeness relation. A closer look makes the completeness relation evident because of the fact that sum of probabilities over all possible outcomes has to be 1.

A special case of the general measurements described above are the projective measurements. A projective measurement is defined by a set of operators $\{P_i = M_i^{\dagger} M_i\}$ that satisfy two conditions; the completeness relation, i.e, $\sum_i P_i = 1$ and that the operators are orthogonal, i.e, $P_i P_{i'} = P_i$ only when $i = i'$.

The measurement defined by the set of operators

$$C_m = \{|00\rangle \langle 00| \, , |01\rangle \langle 01| \, , |10\rangle \langle 10| \, , |11\rangle \langle 11|\}$$

is an example of the projective measurement.

In the next three sections, we will introduce a few interesting applications that use entanglement as the weapon of its choice to demonstrate and achieve something that is otherwise inconceivable in the classical setting.

## 1.7 Quantum Teleportation

Imagine the following scenario. Alice and Bob are friends. Alice has a secret quantum state $|\psi\rangle = \alpha|0\rangle + \beta|1\rangle$ that she wants to send to Bob. Unfortunately, she has access only to a classical channel and not a quantum channel. Will she be able to send the state to Bob? Well, she cannot. But, she then remembers that a long time ago when Alice and Bob met up together, they made an entangled pair and as a souvenir, Alice took one of the entangled qubits and gave Bob the other qubit. Will this be of any use to her in sending the quantum state to Bob? Well, quantum teleportation comes to her rescue.

The idea of quantum teleportation was first proposed by Bennett et al. They described a method that would completely de-construct a quantum state and then reconstruct the same state using just the classical information and the non-classical correlations in the EPR pairs. The quantum teleportation protocol is executed using the circuit in Fig. 1.6.

In Fig. 1.6, the subscripts 0 and 1 with Alice indicate that Alice possesses two particles; labeled as particle 0 and particle 1. Alice essentially brings together the state $|\psi\rangle = \alpha|0\rangle + \beta|1\rangle$ (particle 0) and the entangled particle she has (particle 1) and measures them in the Bell basis. Bell basis is the basis for two qubits systems that contains the four Bell states. She then transmits the two bit output, say $b_0 b_1$, to Bob through the classical channel. Once Bob receives the two bits output, he applies an X gate on his qubit that was entangled to the Alice's qubit if $b_1$ is 1 and then applies Z gate if $b_0$ is 1.

To understand why quantum teleportation works, let us first chart out the evolution of the system with the application of the gates. We will use the subscript 0,1 and 2 to mark the qubits. At the very first beginning, when Alice and Bob were together, they had applied the following unitaries on qubits 1 and 2 to create the entanglement. Then Bob went with qubit 2 and Alice stayed back with qubit 1.

**Fig. 1.6** Circuit for quantum teleportation

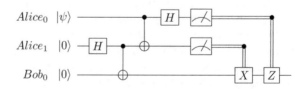

**Table 1.1** The possible scenarios of the qubits of Alice and Bob once Alice measures her qubits in the computational basis

| State Alice observes | State of Bob's qubit |
|---|---|
| $|00\rangle$ | $\alpha|0\rangle + \beta|1\rangle$ |
| $|01\rangle$ | $\beta|0\rangle + \alpha|1\rangle$ |
| $|10\rangle$ | $\alpha|0\rangle - \beta|1\rangle$ |
| $|11\rangle$ | $\beta|0\rangle - \alpha|1\rangle$ |

$$|\psi\rangle_0 |0\rangle_1 |0\rangle_2 \xrightarrow{I_0 \otimes H_1 \otimes I_2} \frac{1}{\sqrt{2}} |\psi\rangle_0 (|0\rangle + |1\rangle)_1 |0\rangle_2$$

$$\xrightarrow{I_0 \otimes CNOT_{1,2}} \frac{1}{\sqrt{2}} |\psi\rangle_0 (|0\rangle|0\rangle + |1\rangle|1\rangle)_{12}$$

$$= \frac{1}{\sqrt{2}} (\alpha|0\rangle + \beta|1\rangle)_0 (|00\rangle + |11\rangle)_{12}$$

$$= \frac{1}{\sqrt{2}} (\alpha|000\rangle_{012} + \alpha|011\rangle_{012} + \beta|100\rangle_{012} + \beta|111\rangle_{012}).$$

This part is for preparing the entanglement. At some later point in time, Alice performs the following operations to teleport the intended state $|\psi\rangle$.

$$\xrightarrow{CNOT_{0,1} \otimes I_2} \frac{1}{\sqrt{2}} (\alpha|0\rangle_0 |00\rangle_{12} + \alpha|0\rangle_0 |11\rangle_{12} + \beta|1\rangle_0 |10\rangle_{12} + \beta|1\rangle_0 |01\rangle_{12})$$

$$\xrightarrow{H_0 \otimes I_1 \otimes I_2} \frac{1}{2} [\alpha(|0\rangle + |1\rangle)_0 |00\rangle_{12} + \alpha(|0\rangle + |1\rangle)_0 |11\rangle_{12} +$$

$$\beta(|0\rangle - |1\rangle)_0 |10\rangle_{12} + \beta(|0\rangle - |1\rangle)_0 |01\rangle_{12}]$$

$$= \frac{1}{2} \Big[ |00\rangle_{01} (\alpha|0\rangle + \beta|1\rangle)_2 + |01\rangle_{01} (\beta|0\rangle + \alpha|1\rangle)_2 +$$

$$|10\rangle_{01} (\alpha|0\rangle - \beta|1\rangle)_2 + |11\rangle_{01} (\beta|0\rangle - \alpha|1\rangle)_2 \Big].$$

The possible scenarios of the qubits with Alice and Bob after Alice measures the qubits with her in the computational basis are depicted in Table 1.1.

So, when Alice measures the first two qubits, Bob's qubit collapses to one of the four possible superpositions. In each case, on applying the conditional X gate and conditional Z gate on Bob's qubit, we can easily observe that the state of the Bob's qubit changes to $|\psi\rangle$ which Alice intended to send Bob.

Let us now look at the Qiskit implementation of the quantum teleportation algorithm. Consider the following code.

```
1 #Importing the classes and modules
2 from qiskit import *
3
4 #Creating quantum register, classical register
```

```
5  #and quantum circuit.
6  q = QuantumRegister(3)
7  ca = ClassicalRegister(2)
8  cb = ClassicalRegister(1)
9  qc = QuantumCircuit(q,ca,cb)
10
11 #Creating entanglement between the qubits q[1] and q
      [2].
12 qc.h(q[1])
13 qc.cx(q[1],q[2])
14
15 #Creating a dummy state in qubit q[0] that is to be
16 #teleported.
17 qc.h(q[0])
18
19 #CNOT and H gates applied by Alice followed by
20 #measurement.
21 qc.cx(q[0],q[1])
22 qc.h(q[0])
23 qc.measure(q[0],ca[0])
24 qc.measure(q[1],ca[1])
25 qc.barrier()
26
27 #Controlled on the output received by Bob,
28 #he performs X gate and Z gate.
29 qc.x(q[2]).c_if(ca[1],1)
30 qc.z(q[2]).c_if(ca[0],1)
31
32 #Performing a check if the state obtained is the
33 #one intended to be teleported.
34 qc.h(q[2])
35 qc.measure(q[2],cb[0])
36
37 #Executing the circuit in the simulator
38 backend = Aer.get_backend('qasm_simulator')
39 qjob = execute(qc,backend)
40 counts = qjob.result().get_counts()
41 print(counts)
```

**Listing 1.13** Qiskit code to demonstrate quantum teleportation

```
1 Output:
2 {'0 11': 249, '0 01': 277, '0 10': 244, '0 00': 254}
```

Note that teleportation is a non-local phenomenon. Implementation of teleportation is useful if we have two parties at two different places and one of the parties intend to send a quantum state to the other. However, the above code will run in a single processor and is just a simulation of teleportation in a quantum computational environment.

In the code, we consider a quantum register with three qubits (q), a classical register (ca) with two bits for Alice and a classical register (cb) with one bit for Bob.

Line 12 and 13 implement the generation of entanglement between the qubits q[1] and q[2] in the circuit qc. In line 16, Hadamard gate is applied on q[0] to evolve the state to $\frac{1}{\sqrt{2}}(|0\rangle + |1\rangle)$. Here, q[0] is $|\psi\rangle$ which Alice aims to teleport. Note that this is just an example state to be teleported. To teleport an arbitrary state, we could create any arbitrary state of our choice with a $U_3$ gate discussed earlier. In lines 19 and 20 we have the code for Alice's operations on the qubit 0 and 1. First, she applies CNOT in the circuit, qc, with q[0] as control and q[1] as target followed by Hadamard (h) operation on q[1]. Code in lines 21 and 22 performs measurement of Alice's qubits. The measurement result on measuring q[0] is stored in ca[0] and the measurement result on measuring q[1] is stored in ca[1]. The command qc.barrier() separates between the operations of Alice and that of Bob as we are simulating the operations together in a single processor but which are supposed to be happening in different places. Next, Bob's operations are performed in lines 29 and 30. The syntax qc.x(q[2]).c_if(ca[1],1) implies that Bob will apply X gate on q[2], if ca[1] = 1. Similarly, he will apply Z on q[2]  if ca[0] = 1.

To check the correctness of the obtained state, we perform the inverse of the operations that were applied on $|0\rangle$ to create the state that was supposed to be teleported. In our case the teleported state is $H|0\rangle = |+\rangle$. Hence, we apply $H^\dagger$ (line 34). If the teleported state is indeed $|\psi\rangle$, then the state would be $H^\dagger|+\rangle = H|+\rangle = |0\rangle$ and we would always obtain $|0\rangle$ on measuring the final state. In line 35, measurement is performed on q[2] and the measurement result is stored in cb[0]. We execute the program in 'qasm_simulator' and use the default number of shots, i.e, 1024 shots.

In the output, the first bit contains the measurement of the qubit q[2], i.e., cb[0] and the next two bits contain the measurement outcomes of the qubits q[0] and q[1], i.e, ca[0] and ca[1] respectively in the ordering (ca[1] ca[0]). From the output we can observe that as expected we have obtained $|0\rangle$ as the measurement output in all the samples indicating that the correct state has been teleported.

Quantum teleportation is an excellent tool that exhibits the power of quantum entanglement. It is an important resource for quantum communication. It also illustrates how information can be transferred from one place to another with just a classical channel and a pre-shared entangled pair.

## 1.8  Superdense Coding

Superdense coding is a quantum technique that uses quantum entanglement to achieve a transmission of two bits of information by sending just a single qubit. This technique was first introduced by Bennett and Wiesner. Suppose Alice wants to send two bits of classical information to Bob. But she is restricted to sending only a single bit or a single qubit. Obviously sending just a single bit is not a solution to the problem.

**Fig. 1.7** Quantum circuit for superdense coding

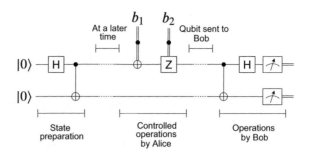

But if she has an entangled pair shared with Bob, she can use super-dense coding to achieve the goal.

The protocol is as follows. Let the two bits of message she aims to send Bob be $b_1 b_2$. If $b_1$ is 1, Alice applies an X gate to her qubit of the entangled pair and then if $b_2$ is 1, she applies a Z gate to her qubit. The evolution of the states of the two qubits due to these operations is given below and the corresponding quantum circuit is illustrated in Fig. 1.7.

$$\frac{1}{\sqrt{2}}(|00\rangle + |11\rangle) \xrightarrow{cX \otimes I} \frac{1}{\sqrt{2}}(|b_1\rangle |0\rangle + |\overline{b_1}\rangle |1\rangle)$$

$$\xrightarrow{cZ \otimes I} \frac{1}{\sqrt{2}}\left((-1)^{b_2 \cdot b_1} |b_1\rangle |0\rangle + (-1)^{b_2 \cdot \overline{b_1}} |\overline{b_1}\rangle |1\rangle\right)$$

Here $\overline{b_1}$ implies the complement of the bit $b_1$.

Once these operations are performed, Alice sends her qubit to Bob. Bob on receiving Alice's qubit applies *CNOT* on his qubit controlled on the received qubit and then applies a H gate on the received qubit. These operations evolve the system as

$$\frac{1}{\sqrt{2}}\left((-1)^{b_2 \cdot b_1} |b_1\rangle |0\rangle + (-1)^{b_2 \cdot \overline{b_1}} |\overline{b_1}\rangle |1\rangle\right) \xrightarrow{cX_{1,2}} \frac{1}{\sqrt{2}}\left[(-1)^{b_2 \cdot b_1} |b_1\rangle + \right.$$
$$\left. (-1)^{b_2 \cdot \overline{b_1}} |\overline{b_1}\rangle\right] |b_1\rangle$$
$$\xrightarrow{H \otimes I} |b_2\rangle |b_1\rangle .$$

Hence, on measuring the qubits, Bob obtains the message bits $b_1 b_2$.

As an example, consider a scenario where Alice wishes to send the message $b_1 b_2 = 11$ to Bob. She has the entangled pair $|\psi\rangle = \frac{1}{\sqrt{2}}(|00\rangle + |11\rangle)$ shared with Bob. To send the message, she first performs an X gate on her qubit since $b_1 = 1$. So the state of the entangled pair transforms as

$$\frac{1}{\sqrt{2}}(|00\rangle + |11\rangle) \xrightarrow{X \otimes I} \frac{1}{\sqrt{2}}(|10\rangle + |01\rangle).$$

Alice then applies a Z gate on her qubit since $b_2 = 1$. Then, the resulting transformation would be

$$\frac{1}{\sqrt{2}}(|10\rangle + |01\rangle) \xrightarrow{Z \otimes I} \frac{1}{\sqrt{2}}(-|10\rangle + |01\rangle).$$

She then sends her qubit to Bob. Bob then applies $CNOT$ and H evolving the state as

$$\frac{1}{\sqrt{2}}(-|10\rangle + |01\rangle \xrightarrow{CNOT_{0,1}} \frac{1}{\sqrt{2}}(-|11\rangle + |01\rangle)$$

$$= \frac{1}{\sqrt{2}}(|0\rangle - |1\rangle)|1\rangle = |-\rangle|1\rangle$$

$$\xrightarrow{H \otimes I} |1\rangle|1\rangle.$$

Bob on measuring the final state obtains the outcome 11 with probability 1.

We have seen the math behind the super-dense coding, let us now simulate it in Qiskit. Remember that just like teleportation, for a useful implementation of super dense coding, we need two parties at two different places with the ability to send and receive qubits. The following code simulates the super-dense coding where the message bits '11' are being transmitted.

```
1  #Importing the classes and modules
2  from qiskit import *
3
4  #Creating quantum register, classical register
5  #and quantum circuit.
6  q = QuantumRegister(2)
7  c = ClassicalRegister(2)
8  qc = QuantumCircuit(q,c)
9
10 #Creating entanglement between the qubits q[0] and q
       [1]
11 qc.h(q[0])
12 qc.cx(q[0],q[1])
13
14 #Alice applying the controlled operations on q[0]
15 qc.x(0)
16 qc.z(0)
17
18 #Bob applying the CNOT and H operations
19 qc.cx(q[0],q[1])
20 qc.h(q[0])
21
22 #Measuring the qubits to obtain the message
23 qc.measure(q[0],c[1])
24 qc.measure(q[1],c[0])
25
26 #Executing the circuit in the simulator
27 backend = Aer.get_backend('qasm_simulator')
28 qjob = execute(qc,backend)
```

```
29  counts  =  qjob.result().get_counts()
30  print(counts)
```
**Listing 1.14** Qiskit code for superdense coding

```
1  Output:
2  {'11':  1024}
```

In the code, we consider one quantum register q of two qubits and one classical register c of two bits. q[0] and q[1] represent the qubits in the entangled pair and are each with Alice and Bob, respectively. In line 11 and 12, we create an entanglement between the qubit q[0] of Alice and the qubit q[1] of Bob. Since the message to be transmitted was '11', both the X gate and the Z gate were applied on qubit q[0] by Alice. Observe that in line 15 and 16, unlike earlier code, we write qc.x(0) and qc.z(0) instead of qc.x(q[0]) and qc.z(q[0]). A point to note is that both the syntaxes performs the same task and can be used interchangeably. Line 19 and 20 describe Bob's operations on the qubits q[0] and q[1]. Measurement results are stored in the bits c[0] and c[1]. On measuring the final state, we can observe from the output that we obtain 11 with probability 1.

Despite the fact that two qubits are involved, the sender essentially interacts using just a single qubit to convey two bits of classical information. Superdense coding is a neat example that illustrates the power of quantum information processing.

## 1.9   CHSH Game

In this section, we demonstrate the power of quantum entanglement with a game. In this game there are three parties; Alice, Bob and Charlie. Alice and Bob are players whereas Charlie serves as a referee. The rules of the game are as follows. In each round of the game, Charlie chooses two bits $x$ and $y$ uniformly and independently at random and then gives $x$ to Alice and $y$ to Bob. After getting the inputs, Alice and Bob are not allowed to communicate amongst themselves. On receipt of the input bits, Alice sends an output bit $a$ to Charlie and Bob sends an output bit $b$ to Charlie. Alice and Bob win the game if they can ensure that:

$$x \cdot y = a \oplus b.$$

Here, $\oplus$ means addition modulo 2. In a classical setting, the best Alice and Bob can do is to output $a = 0$ and $b = 0$ (or $a = 1, b = 1$) no matter what the input bits $x$ and $y$ are. Since $x \cdot y$ is 0 for three out of the four possible combinations, Alice and Bob will win the game with a probability 0.75. Can they do better than this? Unfortunately, in a classical setting this is the optimal strategy. However, quantum entanglement keeps their hopes high. If they can share a pair of entangled qubits before the game starts, they can win the game with a better success probability. The quantum strategy they would follow is explained next.

Alice and Bob will share a maximally entangled state, i.e, the Bell state of the form $\frac{1}{\sqrt{2}}(|0\rangle|0\rangle + |1\rangle|1\rangle)$. If Alice receives $x = 0$, she will measure her qubit and if $x = 1$, she applies a $U_3(\frac{\pi}{2}, 0, \pi)$ rotation to her qubit and then measure it. Note that the measurements are performed in the computational basis. If she obtains $|0\rangle$ on measurement, she will output $a = 0$ and 1 otherwise. Alice then sends the output bit $a$ to Charlie.

On the other side, if Bob receives $y = 0$, he applies a $U_3(\frac{-\pi}{4}, 0, 0)$ rotation to his qubit and if he receives $y = 1$, he applies a $U_3(\frac{\pi}{4}, 0, 0)$ rotation to his qubit. He then measures the qubit in the computational basis and will output $b = 0$ if he gets $|0\rangle$ as the measurement outcome and 1 otherwise. Bob then sends the output to Charlie.

Let us now analyze the winning probability of this strategy. We have four possible cases of inputs and the corresponding actions of Alice and Bob. Note that Alice and Bob win the game if they output $ab \in \{00, 11\}$ when the input is $xy \in \{00, 01, 10\}$ and if they output $ab \in \{01, 10\}$ when the input is $xy = 11$. Now, we analyze each of the four cases.

**Case(i): xy = 00.** In this case Alice just measures her qubit and Bob applies $U_3(\frac{-\pi}{4}, 0, 0)$ to his qubit and measures. The evolution of the states of their qubits will be as follows.

$$\frac{1}{\sqrt{2}}(|00\rangle + |11\rangle) \xrightarrow{I \otimes U_3(\frac{-\pi}{4},0,0)} \frac{1}{\sqrt{2}}\Big[ |0\rangle (\cos\frac{\pi}{8}|0\rangle - \sin\frac{\pi}{8}|1\rangle)$$
$$+ |1\rangle (\sin\frac{\pi}{8}|0\rangle + \cos\frac{\pi}{8}|1\rangle))\Big]$$
$$= \frac{1}{\sqrt{2}}\Big[ \cos\frac{\pi}{8}|00\rangle - \sin\frac{\pi}{8}|01\rangle + \sin\frac{\pi}{8}|10\rangle + \cos\frac{\pi}{8}|11\rangle \Big].$$

From the final state, we can see that the probability of winning is

$$Pr(win) = Pr(|00\rangle) + Pr(|11\rangle) = \frac{1}{2}\Big[ \cos^2\frac{\pi}{8} + \cos^2\frac{\pi}{8} \Big] = \cos^2\frac{\pi}{8} \approx 0.854.$$

**Case (ii): xy = 01.** Alice and Bob will win the game in this case if they again output 00 or 11. Similar to case(i), Alice just measures but Bob now applies $U_3(\frac{\pi}{4}, 0, 0)$ to his qubit and measures. To obtain the probability of $win$, let use first look at the evolution of the system which is as follows.

$$\frac{1}{\sqrt{2}}(|00\rangle + |11\rangle) \xrightarrow{I \otimes U_3(\frac{\pi}{4},0,0)} \frac{1}{\sqrt{2}}\Big[ |0\rangle (\cos\frac{\pi}{8}|0\rangle + \sin\frac{\pi}{8}|1\rangle)$$
$$+ |1\rangle (-\sin\frac{\pi}{8}|0\rangle + \cos\frac{\pi}{8}|1\rangle))\Big]$$
$$= \frac{1}{\sqrt{2}}\Big[ \cos\frac{\pi}{8}|00\rangle + \sin\frac{\pi}{8}|01\rangle - \sin\frac{\pi}{8}|10\rangle + \cos\frac{\pi}{8}|11\rangle \Big].$$

Hence, the probability of winning in this case is

$$Pr(win) = Pr(|00\rangle) + Pr(|11\rangle) = \frac{1}{2}\left[\cos^2\frac{\pi}{8} + \cos^2\frac{\pi}{8}\right] = \cos^2\frac{\pi}{8} \approx 0.854.$$

**Case (iii): xy = 10.** Note that, in this case, $x = 1$. So, Alice applies a $U_3(\frac{\pi}{2}, 0, \pi)$ gate to her qubit and Bob applies a $U_3(-\frac{\pi}{4}, 0, 0)$ gate to his qubit before measurement. This evolves the states of their qubits as

$$\frac{1}{\sqrt{2}}(|00\rangle + |11\rangle) \xrightarrow{U_3(\frac{\pi}{2},0,\pi)\otimes U_3(\frac{-\pi}{4},0,0)} \frac{1}{2}\Big[(|0\rangle + |1\rangle)(\cos\frac{\pi}{8}|0\rangle - \sin\frac{\pi}{8}|1\rangle)$$
$$+ (|0\rangle - |1\rangle)(\sin\frac{\pi}{8}|0\rangle + \cos\frac{\pi}{8}|1\rangle)\Big]$$
$$= \frac{1}{2}\Big[(\cos\frac{\pi}{8} + \sin\frac{\pi}{8})|00\rangle + (-\sin\frac{\pi}{8} + \cos\frac{\pi}{8})|01\rangle$$
$$+ (\cos\frac{\pi}{8} - \sin\frac{\pi}{8})|10\rangle + (-\sin\frac{\pi}{8} - \cos\frac{\pi}{8})|11\rangle\Big].$$

This gives us the probability of winning as

$$Pr(win) = \frac{1}{4}\left[\left(\cos\frac{\pi}{8} + \sin\frac{\pi}{8}\right)^2 + \left(-\sin\frac{\pi}{8} - \cos\frac{\pi}{8}\right)^2\right]$$
$$= \frac{1}{2}\left(\cos\frac{\pi}{8} + \sin\frac{\pi}{8}\right)^2 = \frac{1}{2}\left(1 + \sin\frac{\pi}{4}\right) \approx 0.854.$$

**Case (iv): xy = 11.** In this case Alice applies the $U_3(\frac{\pi}{2}, 0, \pi)$ gate to her qubit and Bob applies $U_3(\frac{\pi}{4}, 0, 0)$ to his qubit and they measure. The evolution of their states look like the following.

$$\frac{1}{\sqrt{2}}(|00\rangle + |11\rangle) \xrightarrow{U_3(\frac{\pi}{2},0,\pi)\otimes U_3(\frac{\pi}{4},0,0)} \frac{1}{2}\Big[(|0\rangle + |1\rangle)(\cos\frac{\pi}{8}|0\rangle + \sin\frac{\pi}{8}|1\rangle)$$
$$+ (|0\rangle - |1\rangle)(-\sin\frac{\pi}{8}|0\rangle + \cos\frac{\pi}{8}|1\rangle)\Big]$$
$$= \frac{1}{2}\Big[(\cos\frac{\pi}{8} - \sin\frac{\pi}{8})|00\rangle + (\sin\frac{\pi}{8} + \cos\frac{\pi}{8})|01\rangle$$
$$+ (\cos\frac{\pi}{8} + \sin\frac{\pi}{8})|10\rangle + (\sin\frac{\pi}{8} - \cos\frac{\pi}{8})|11\rangle\Big].$$

Remember that to win the game in this case, Alice and Bob need to output $ab = 01$ or $ab = 10$. Hence, the probability of winning is obtained as

$$Pr(win) = \frac{1}{4}\left[\left(\sin\frac{\pi}{8} + \cos\frac{\pi}{8}\right)^2 + \left(\cos\frac{\pi}{8} + \sin\frac{\pi}{8}\right)^2\right]$$
$$= \frac{1}{2}\left(\cos\frac{\pi}{8} + \sin\frac{\pi}{8}\right)^2 = \frac{1}{2}\left(1 + \sin\frac{\pi}{4}\right) \approx 0.854.$$

Observed that in all the cases, the probability of winning is $\approx 0.854$ which is much greater than that of the classical strategies. This is a strong result that highlights the power of quantum entanglement. This result also conveys that the correlation between qubits achievable from quantum entanglement is not possible in a classical setting.

Next, let us simulate the CHSH game in Qiskit and check if practical results coincide with the theoretical expectations. Here, we would like to emphasize the word "simulation" as the CHSH game is non-local and three spatially separated parties are required in reality which is not possible in Qiskit. The Qiskit code for CHSH game is given below. In the code one may find the use of the `barrier()` command multiple times. This command is used to distinguish the actions of three different parties; Alice, Bob and Charlie.

```
 1 #Importing the classes and modules
 2 from qiskit import *
 3 from math import pi
 4
 5 #Creating quantum register, classical register
 6 #and quantum circuit
 7 qin = QuantumRegister(2)
 8 qout = QuantumRegister(2)
 9 cin = ClassicalRegister(2)
10 cout = ClassicalRegister(2)
11 qc = QuantumCircuit(qin,qout,cin,cout)
12
13 #Pre-game preparation of entanglement
14 #between qubits qout[0] and qout[1]
15 qc.h(qout[0])
16 qc.cx(qout[0],qout[1])
17 qc.barrier()
18
19 #Charlie obtains x,y uniformly and independently at
20 #random
21 qc.h([qin[0],qin[1]])
22 qc.measure(qin[0],cin[1]) #This is x
23 qc.measure(qin[1],cin[0]) #This is y
24 qc.barrier()
25
26 #Depending on the state of x Alice performs her
27 #operation.
28 qc.cu3(pi/2,0,pi,qin[0],qout[0])
29 qc.measure(qout[0],cout[1])
30
31 #Depending on the state of y Bob performs his
32 #operations.
33 #We put X-gate because we want the below gate to be
34 #applied only if qin=0. So we use X(qin) as control.
35 qc.x(qin[1])
36 qc.cu3(-pi/4,0,0,qin[1],qout[1])
37 qc.x(qin[1])
38 qc.cu3(pi/4,0,0,qin[1],qout[1])
39 qc.measure(qout[1],cout[0])
40
41 #Creating and running the job in the machine.
42 backend = Aer.get_backend("qasm_simulator")
```

```
43 qjob = execute(qc,backend=backend,shots=1024)
44 result = qjob.result()
45 stats = result.get_counts()
46
47 #Measure the winning percentage
48 won = 0
49 lost = 0
50 for dat in stats:
51     if (int(dat[3])*int(dat[4]))==((int(dat[0])+int(
    dat[1]))%2): # Check if the condition is satisfied.
52         won += stats[dat]
53     else:
54         lost += stats[dat]
55 print("The number of games won : ", won)
56 print("The number of games lost : ", lost)
```

**Listing 1.15** Qiskit code for CHSH game

```
1 Output:
2 The number of games won: 880
3 The number of games lost: 144
```

In the code above, we used two quantum registers named qin and qout. Each consists of two qubits. The two qubits in qin will be accessed by Charlie and the two qubits at qout will be accessed by Alice and Bob, one qubit each. The quantum registers qin and qout are associated with the classical registers cin and cout respectively. The code written in the lines 15 and 16 is for generation of an entanglement between the qubit with Alice and that with Bob. Alice gets to access qout[0] and Bob gets to access qout[1].

Recall that Charlie obtains $x, y$ uniformly and independently at random. We use Hadamard gates on qin[0] and qin[1] and measure these two qubits to simulate this behaviour (line 21, 22 and 23). To understand this operation we refer the reader to Sect. 1.3. The measurement result for qin[0] is stored in cin[1], which will be used as $x$ and the measurement result for qin[1] is stored in cin[0] which will be used as $y$.

Lines 28 and 29 describe the actions of Alice. In the code, a controlled-$U_3(\pi/2, 0, \pi)$ gate is applied on qin[0] and qout[0] with qin[0] as control and qout[0] as target. However, in reality as qin[0] would be with Charlie, qout[0] with Alice and they are spatially separated, the controlled gate simulates the behaviour that Alice conditionally applies the $U_3(-\pi/2, 0, \pi)$ gate to her qubit depending on the value of the bit she receives from Charlie. If qin[0]= 1, $U_3(\pi/2, 0, \pi)$ will be in action. The measurement result for qout[0] will be stored at cout[1] which will be used as $a$.

Code in lines 35 to 39 perform the action of Bob's operations in a similar manner. Bob applies $U_3(-\pi/4, 0, 0)$ on qout[1] if qin[1]= 0 and $U_3(\pi/4, 0, 0)$ on qout[1] if qin[1]= 1. In general , a controlled gate will be in action when its controlled bit is 1. Here, for the first case, the condition is reversed, i.e, we need to perform the operation if the controlled bit is 0. To perform the same, we use an X gate on the controlled qubit qin[1] so that when qin[1] is 0, X gate flips the value and

$U_3(-\pi/4, 0, 0)$ will be in action. This is followed by another X gate that turns back `qin[1]` to its original state. Note that the state of `qin[1]` remains the same when applying the `cu3(`$\pi$`/4,0,0)` gate at line 38 and hence $U3(\pi/4, 0, 0)$ gets applied on `qout[1]` if and only if `qin[1]` is 1. The measurement result for `qout[1]` is stored in `cout[0]`. Here, the counts are stored in `stats`. The variable `won` and `lost` are initialized at 0. Line 51 checks whether the condition $x \cdot y = a \oplus b$ is satisfied. If the condition is satisfied, `won` is increased by 1, if not then `lost` is increased by 1. In our experiments, the game has been won 880 times out 1024. this provides a rough estimate of the winning probability of the game as $\frac{880}{1024} \approx 0.859$.

**Further Reading**

The history of quantum computing is difficult to trace since it started as an application of quantum mechanics which itself has a remarkable and fascinating journey even since it was proposed. A quantum computer that can be programmed in the modern sense of the word was first proposed by David Deutsch [4]. He laid down the specifications and operational principles of a general purpose quantum computer, the so-called "quantum universal Turing machine". The architecture that he followed is functionally similar to what is currently known as the "gate model" of quantum computers. Most early initiatives to develop hardware for quantum computing focused on the "gate model" in which the operations are programmed at a low-level using a set of unitary gates. The IBM Quantum platform also follows the same architecture and all the sample programs given in this book are also written in the same.

For a thorough understanding of quantum computing one may consult the book "Quantum Computation and Quantum Information" by Nielsen and Chuang [8]. The no-cloning theorem is one of the early limitations programmers may face since it does not allow them to create (temporary) copies of variables holding arbitrary quantum states, something that is done routinely in programs written for classical computers. This theorem was first stated and then proved by Wootters, Zurek and Dieks in 1982 [5, 9]; a simplified proof can be found in the book mentioned above by Nielsen and Chuang [8].

Quantum teleportation is one of the earliest fascinating results on quantum computing. It was proposed by Bennett et al. [1]. Bennett and Wiesner also proposed superdense coding protocol [2]. The idea of CHSH game follows from the seminal work of Clauser et al [3]. The optimality of 0.75 as the maximum winning probability using classical strategies was proved by Cirel'son et al. in [10].

# References

1. Bennett, C.H., Brassard, G., Crépeau, C., Jozsa, R., Peres, A., Wootters, W.K.: Teleporting an unknown quantum state via dual classical and Einstein-Podolsky-Rosen channels. Phys. Rev. Lett. **70**(13), 1895 (1993)
2. Bennett, C.H., Wiesner, S.J.: Communication via one-and two-particle operators on Einstein-Podolsky-Rosen states. Phys. Rev. Lett. **69**(20), 2881 (1992)

3. Clauser, J.F., Horne, M.A., Shimony, A., Holt, R.A.: Proposed experiment to test local hidden-variable theories. Phys. Rev. Lett. **23**(15), 880–4 (1969)
4. Deutsch, D.: Quantum theory, the Church-Turing principle and the universal quantum computer. Proc. R. Soc. Lond. A. Math. Phys. Sci. **400**(1818), 97–117 (1985)
5. Dieks, D.: Communication by EPR devices. Phys. Lett. A **92**(6), 271–272 (1982)
6. IBM Q. IBM Quantum Experience. https://quantum-computing.ibm.com/
7. IBM Q Wiki Page. https://en.wikipedia.org/wiki/IBM_Q_Experience
8. Nielsen, M.A., Chuang, I.L.: Quantum Computation and Quantum Information, Anniversary, 10th edn. Cambridge University Press, USA (2011)
9. Wootters, W., Zurek, W.: A single quantum cannot be cloned. Nature **299**, 802–803 (1982)
10. Cirel'son, B.S.: Quantum generalizations of Bell's inequality. Lett. Math. Phys. **4**(2), 93–100 (1980)

# Chapter 2
# Deutsch-Jozsa and Walsh Spectrum

**Abstract** In this chapter we study the well known Deutsch-Jozsa algorithm and relate it with the Walsh spectrum of a Boolean function. We first introduce the basics of Boolean functions and then proceed with the quantum algorithms that deal with them. Different scenarios are presented to show how the Walsh spectrum of a Boolean function evolves during the execution of the Deutsch-Jozsa and other related algorithms. Necessary implementations in the Qiskit SDK are also presented.

**Keywords** Boolean functions · Bernstein-Vazirani algorithm · Deutsch and Deutsch-Jozsa algorithms · Walsh transform

## 2.1 Boolean Functions

Boolean functions are the fundamental elements of many fields like cryptography, coding theory and learning theory.

> **Definition 2.1.1: Boolean Function**
>
> An $n$-bit input, $m$-bit output Boolean function is a mapping $f : \{0, 1\}^n \longrightarrow \{0, 1\}^m$.

For the sake of simplicity, a Boolean function with an $m$-bit output can be perceived as $m$ different Boolean functions of the form $f_i : \{0, 1\}^n \longrightarrow \{0, 1\}$. Hence, from here on, we will mostly concentrate on the $n$-bit input, 1-bit output Boolean functions unless explicitly mentioned. A Boolean function can be represented in various forms. The truth table of a Boolean function is a table containing all possible combinations of the input values and their corresponding outputs. For instance, the truth table of the two bit $AND$ function is given in Fig. 2.1.

The list consisting of all the $2^n$ outputs of an $n$-bit Boolean function $f$, given as

© The Author(s), under exclusive license to Springer Nature Singapore Pte Ltd. 2021　　39
T. SAPV et al., *Quantum Algorithms for Cryptographically Significant Boolean Functions*,
SpringerBriefs in Computer Science,
https://doi.org/10.1007/978-981-16-3061-3_2

**Fig. 2.1** Various
representations of AND
function

| x  | f(x) |
|----|------|
| 00 | 0    |
| 01 | 0    |
| 10 | 0    |
| 11 | 1    |

$$f(x) = x_1 \cdot x_2 = x_1 \wedge x_2$$

$$f = \left[ f(i) : 0 \leq i \leq 2^n - 1 \right],$$

is called the truth-table representation of the function $f$, where $i$ denotes the decimal representation of the input string and $f(i)$ denotes the corresponding output of the Boolean function $f$. It is to be noted that the $f(i)$ values in the list is arranged as per the numeric order of the inputs $i$. For the 2-bit $AND$ function, the complete truth table representation is given as $f = [f(00), f(01), f(10), f(11)] = [0, 0, 0, 1]$. Another form of representation of a Boolean function is the Algebraic Normal Form (ANF).

---

**Definition 2.1.2: Algebraic Normal Form**

Any $n$-variate Boolean function can be considered an $n$-variate polynomial over the finite field $GF(2)$. More formally, this polynomial can be written as

$$a_0 \bigoplus_{1 \leq i \leq n} a_i x_i \bigoplus_{1 \leq i < j \leq n} a_{ij} x_i x_j \bigoplus \cdots \bigoplus a_{12 \cdots n} x_1 x_2 \cdots x_n,$$

where $a_i, a_{ij}, \cdots, a_{12 \cdots n}$ are the coefficients that are either 0 or 1. Here, $\oplus$ means addition modulo 2. The number of variables present in the highest order product-term with non-zero coefficients, is called the algebraic degree of the Boolean function.

---

For example, consider the 4-bit Boolean function given by the ANF

$$f(x_1, x_2, x_3, x_4) = 1 \oplus x_1 \oplus x_4 \oplus x_1 x_2 \oplus x_3 x_4 \oplus x_2 x_3 x_4 \oplus x_1 x_2 x_3 x_4.$$

The truth table of this function is presented in Fig. 2.2. We can observe that the algebraic degree of the above Boolean function is 4 since the highest order product term with non-zero coefficient is $x_1 x_2 x_3 x_4$.

It is clear that the functional value at a point can be obtained from the ANF by substituting the values for the variables. Even though it is not very straightforward, it can also be shown that the ANF of a Boolean function can be obtained from its truth table.

Now, we discuss various types of Boolean functions depending on the structure of their truth-table, ANFs, etc.

**Fig. 2.2** Truth-table of the
4-bit Boolean function

| $x$ | $f(x)$ |
|------|--------|
| 0000 | 1 |
| 0001 | 0 |
| 0010 | 1 |
| 0011 | 1 |
| 0100 | 1 |
| 0101 | 0 |
| 0110 | 1 |
| 0111 | 0 |
| 1000 | 0 |
| 1001 | 1 |
| 1010 | 0 |
| 1011 | 0 |
| 1100 | 1 |
| 1101 | 0 |
| 1110 | 1 |
| 1111 | 1 |

**Definition 2.1.3: Non-degeneracy of a Boolean function**

An $n$-bit Boolean function $f(x)$ is said to be non-degenerate on $k$ variables if its ANF contains $k$ distinct variables where $0 \le k \le n$. We say that a Boolean function $f(x)$ is non-degenerate if it is non-degenerate on $n$ variables, i.e., if all the $n$ variables are present in the ANF of $f$.

For instance, the 4-bit Boolean function given by $f(x) = x_1 x_3 \oplus x_4$ is degenerate, as it is non-degenerate on 3 variables only ($x_2$ is absent), whereas the 4-bit Boolean function $f(x) = x_1 \oplus x_3 \oplus x_2 x_4$ is non-degenerate as all the 4 variables are present in its ANF.

**Definition 2.1.4: Homogeneous Boolean function**

A homogeneous Boolean function $f(x)$ is a Boolean function whose ANF contains only terms of the same degree.

The Boolean functions $f(x) = x_1 x_2 \oplus x_3 x_4$ and $f(x) = x_1 \oplus x_2 \oplus x_3$ are examples of homogeneous Boolean functions.

For any binary string $s$, the Hamming weight of $s$, denoted by $wt(s)$, is the number of 1's present in the string. More formally, it is defined as

$$wt(s) = |\{i : s_i = 1\}|$$

where $s_i$ denotes the $i^{th}$ bit of the string $s$. The Hamming distance between two $n$-bit strings $s$ and $t$ is defined as the number of bit positions where $s$ and $t$ differ. It is denoted by $dist(s, t)$. Formally, it can be written as

$$dist(s, t) = |\{i : s_i \neq t_i\}|,$$

where $s_i$ and $t_i$ are the $i^{th}$ bits of the strings $s$ and $t$ respectively. Observe that the Hamming distance is symmetric with respect to $s$ and $t$, and furthermore, the Hamming distance between $s$ and $t$ can also be written as the Hamming weight of the string $s \oplus t$, i.e., $dist(s, t) = wt(s \oplus t)$.

---

**Definition 2.1.5: Balanced Boolean function**

An $n$-variate Boolean function $f(x)$ is said to be balanced if the Hamming weight of the truth table representation of $f$ is $\frac{2^n}{2}$, i.e., $f$ contains equal number of 0's and 1's. Similarly, a Boolean function $f(x)$ is said to be constant if the output of the function is independent of the input bits. In other words, a constant Boolean function is a function such that $f(x) = 1$ for all $x \in \{0, 1\}^n$ or $f(x) = 0$ for all $x \in \{0, 1\}^n$.

---

We will later show that the Deutsch-Jozsa algorithm can distinguish between a constant and a balanced Boolean function more efficiently in quantum domain than the best known algorithm in the classical domain.

---

**Definition 2.1.6: Linear and affine functions**

A Boolean function $f(x)$ is said to be *linear*, if $f(x)$ can be written as

$$f(x) = a \cdot x$$

where $a \cdot x = a_1x_1 \oplus a_2x_2 \oplus \cdots \oplus a_nx_n$. Likewise, a Boolean function $f(x)$ is called *affine*, if it can be written as

$$f(x) = (a \cdot x) \oplus b,$$

where $a \cdot x = a_1x_1 \oplus a_2x_2 \oplus \cdots \oplus a_nx_n$ and $b \in \{0, 1\}$. Note that linear functions are a special case of the affine functions where $b = 0$.

---

Let us consider a 4-bit Boolean function $f(x) = f(x_1, x_2, x_3, x_4) = x_2 \oplus x_3 \oplus x_4$. It is evident that the algebraic degree of the function is 1. The function is non-degenerate on 3 variables and homogeneous. Since $wt(f)$ is $8 = \frac{2^4}{2}$, the function is also balanced. A a keen observation would point out that the function $f(x)$ can also be written as $f(x) = (0111) \cdot x$. Hence the function $f(x)$ is also linear, and so affine.

One of the interesting facts about non-constant affine functions is that they are always balanced. However, the converse need not be true. For, instance the 3-bit Boolean function given by the truth table representation $f = [0, 1, 1, 1, 0, 1, 0, 0]$ is balanced but not an affine function.

In the next few sections, we will look into certain important cryptographic properties of Boolean functions. Study and analysis of these properties will be very crucial
in understanding the security of various ciphers and cryptographic protocols.

## 2.2 Walsh Transform

Walsh transform is one of the most important tools in analysing the cryptographic
properties of Boolean functions.

---

**Definition 2.2.1: Walsh transform**

For an $n$-bit Boolean function $f(x)$, the Walsh transform of $f(x)$ at any point
$a \in \{0, 1\}^n$ is defined as

$$W_f(a) = \sum_{x \in \{0,1\}^n} (-1)^{f(x) \oplus a \cdot x}, \tag{2.1}$$

where $a \cdot x$ denotes the dot product $a_1 x_1 \oplus a_2 x_2 \oplus \cdots \oplus a_n x_n$.

---

The value of the Walsh transform at a point $a$ is called the Walsh coefficient of
$f(x)$ at the point $a$. The Walsh spectrum of the Boolean function $f(x)$ is the list of
all the $2^n$ Walsh coefficients given as

$$W_f = [W_f(0), W_f(1), \cdots, W_f(2^n - 1)],$$

where $W_f(i)$ is the Walsh coefficient at the point whose decimal representation
is given by $i$. There are a few interesting observations in the definition of Walsh
transform. First, notice that the Walsh coefficient at the point $0^{\otimes n}$ can be simplified
to

$$W_f(0^{\otimes n}) = \sum_{x \in \{0,1\}^n} (-1)^{f(x)}.$$

The expression on the right calculates the difference between the number of input
values for which $f(x) = 0$ and those for which $f(x) = 1$. That is,

$$W_f(0^{\otimes n}) = \left| \{x : f(x) = 0\} \right| - \left| \{x : f(x) = 1\} \right| = 2^n - 2wt(f)$$

where $f$ is the truth table representation of $f(x)$. So, for a balanced function, we
have $W_f(0^{\otimes n}) = 0$.

Next, observe the term $f(x) \oplus a \cdot x$. Let $g(x)$ be the defined as $a \cdot x$. Obviously
$g(x)$ is a linear function. Then $f(x) \oplus a \cdot x$ can be written as $h(x) = f(x) \oplus g(x)$.
Notice that, at any specific point $x$, $h(x) = 0$ if $f(x) = g(x)$ and $h(x) = 1$ if $f(x) \neq
g(x)$. Thus, the Walsh coefficient at a point $a$ gives the difference between the number

of points such that $f(x) = a \cdot x$ and the number of points such that $f(x) \neq a \cdot x$. More formally,

$$
\begin{aligned}
W_f(a) &= \left| \{x : f(x) = a \cdot x\} \right| - \left| \{x : f(x) \neq a \cdot x\} \right| \\
&= \left| \{x : h(x) = 0\} \right| - \left| \{x : h(x) = 1\} \right| \\
&= 2^n - 2wt(h),
\end{aligned}
\tag{2.2}
$$

where $h$ is the truth-table representation of the function $h(x) = f(x) \oplus a \cdot x = dist(f, g)$. Thus, the Walsh coefficient at the point $a$ measures the correlation or the distance between the function $f(x)$ and the linear function $a \cdot x$. Note that the Walsh coefficient at a point $a$ not only provides a notion of distance between the function $f(x)$ and the linear function $a \cdot x$, it also provides the distance between the function $f(x)$ and the affine function $(a \cdot x) \oplus 1$. This is due to the fact that if two arbitrary functions $f(x)$ and $g(x)$ agree at $k$ points (i.e., $f(x) = g(x)$ at $k$ many points), then the functions $f(x)$ and $g(x) \oplus 1$ agree at $2^n - k$ many points. So we have

$$
\begin{aligned}
&\left| \{x : f(x) = g(x)\} \right| - \left| \{x : f(x) \neq g(x)\} \right| \\
&= \left| \{x : f(x) \neq g(x) \oplus 1\} \right| - \left| \{x : f(x) = g(x) \oplus 1\} \right|.
\end{aligned}
$$

Using the notion of distance between a function $f(x)$ and the linear functions, we now define the nonlinearity of the function $f(x)$. The nonlinearity of an $n$-bit Boolean function $f(x)$, denoted by $\eta(f)$, is defined as the minimum distance of the function $f(x)$ from the set of all $n$-bit affine functions. Mathematically, it is given as

$$
\eta(f) = min_{g \in \mathcal{A}(n)} \{dist(f, g)\},
$$

where $\mathcal{A}(n)$ is the set of all $n$-bit affine functions. In terms of Walsh spectrum, the nonlinearity of a Boolean function $f(x)$ is defined as

$$
\eta(f) = 2^{n-1} - \frac{1}{2} \max_{a \in \{0,1\}^n} |W_f(a)|.
\tag{2.3}
$$

A very important characteristic of the Walsh spectrum is given by the Parseval's identity. According to this identity, the Walsh coefficients of a Boolean function $f(x)$ satisfy the following identity:

$$
\sum_{a \in \{0,1\}^n} |W_f(a)|^2 = 2^{2n}.
\tag{2.4}
$$

Certain cryptographic properties that are defined using the Walsh transform of a Boolean function, are described below.

---

**Definition 2.2.2: Correlation immunity and Resiliency**

A Boolean function $f(x)$ is said to be correlation immune (CI) of order $k$, if and only if the Walsh transform of $f(x)$ satisfies

$$W_f(a) = 0, \text{ for } 1 \leq wt(a) \leq k.$$

Further, a Boolean function $f(x)$ is called an $m-$resilient function if $f(x)$ is both $m-$CI and balanced. That is, in terms of Walsh coefficients, a function $f(x)$ is $m$-resilient if and only if the Walsh spectrum of $f(x)$ satisfies

$$W_f(a) = 0, \text{ for } 0 \leq wt(a) \leq m.$$

---

## 2.3 Boolean Function Implementation: Classical to Quantum

Before proceeding to the quantum algorithms, we should note that the Boolean functions generally are not bijective. However, given that any quantum gate must be reversible, we should have some mechanism to implement a Boolean function in the quantum domain. In this section, we explain the basic idea to achieve this.

Let $F : \{0, 1\}^n \rightarrow \{0, 1\}^m$ be an $n$-bit input, $m$-bit output Boolean function. Now, we need to implement $F$ in a quantum circuit, but we see that $F$ is not reversible in general. For instance, the AND function $f(x_1, x_2) = x_1 \cdot x_2$ is not reversible since we cannot obtain the input to the function if we are given only its corresponding output value. However, all the gates in a quantum circuit are required to be reversible. To overcome this, a useful concept is that of an oracle function $U_F$. Given a function $F : \{0, 1\}^n \rightarrow \{0, 1\}^m$, the function $U_F$ is an $(n + m)$-input $(n + m)$-output Boolean function that is defined as follows:

$$U_F(x_1, x_2, \cdots, x_n, b) = (x_1, x_2, \cdots, x_n, b \oplus F(x))$$

where $b \in \{0, 1\}^m$ and $x = (x_1, x_2, \cdots, x_n)$.

Now, notice that for any input $x \in \{0, 1\}^n$ obtaining the value of $F(x)$ using $U_F$ is quite straightforward; by setting $b = 0$, the last bit of $U_F(x_1, \cdots, x_n, 0) = (x_1, \cdots, x_n, F(x))$ is the required value. Given an output $y$ of $U_F$, it is always possible to obtain the input of $U_F$ since $U_F(U_F(x_1, \cdots, x_n, b)) = (x_1, \cdots, x_n, b)$; basically $U_F$ retains $(x_1, \cdots, x_n)$ input bits in its output bits which allows one to recover the input from the output of $U_F(x_1, \cdots, x_n, b)$. Unlike $F$, the function $U_F$ is always reversible; further any reversible function can be implemented in a quantum circuit using the universal gate set.

**Table 2.1** Truth-table of $F(x_1, x_2) = x_1 \cdot x_2$ function

| $x_1$ | $x_2$ | $F(x_1, x_2)$ |
|---|---|---|
| 0 | 0 | 0 |
| 0 | 1 | 0 |
| 1 | 0 | 0 |
| 1 | 1 | 1 |

**Table 2.2** Truth-table of the oracle function $U_F$ of $F(x_1, x_2) = x_1 \cdot x_2$

| $x_1$ | $x_2$ | $b$ | $U_F(x_1, x_2, b)$ |
|---|---|---|---|
| 0 | 0 | 0 | 000 |
| 0 | 1 | 0 | 010 |
| 1 | 0 | 0 | 100 |
| 1 | 1 | 0 | 111 |
| 0 | 0 | 1 | 001 |
| 0 | 1 | 1 | 011 |
| 1 | 0 | 1 | 101 |
| 1 | 1 | 1 | 110 |

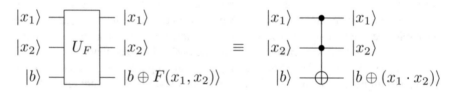

**Fig. 2.3** The quantum circuit of the oracle function $U_F$ for $F(x_1, x_2) = x_1 \cdot x_2$

It is a folklore fact that the number of gates required to implement $U_F$ in a quantum circuit is polynomially related to the number of gates required to implement $F$ in the classical domain.

We now illustrate the ease and importance of $U_F$ with the following example. Let the function $F$ be the AND function, i.e, $F(x_1, x_2) = x_1 \cdot x_2$. Truth table of $F$ is as in Table 2.1. Then, its oracle function $U_F$ is as defined in Table 2.2. It is clearly observable from the Truth Table that the oracle function $U_F$ is bijective. Note that if we were to implement $F$ directly as a quantum circuit, it would not be possible due to its non-reversibility. The corresponding quantum circuit of $U_F$ is as given in Fig. 2.3.

Now, we can code the oracle circuit in Qiskit as below:

```
1 #Importing the required classes and modules
2 from qiskit import *
3
4 #Defining a function that returns the quantum circuit
5 #of the function U_F for the AND function
6 def oracle():
```

```
7      circ = QuantumCircuit(3)
8      circ.ccx(0,1,2)
9      return circ
```

**Listing 2.1** Qiskit code for $U_F$

## 2.4 The Deutsch Algorithm

The Deutsch Algorithm is one of the most simple and one of the first quantum algorithms. Imagine we are provided a 1-bit Boolean function $f(x)$ as a black box. A black box is a model, where the inner functioning is not known, but given an input $x$, the box produces the output $f(x)$. Our goal is to find if the given function is constant or balanced. This problem is called the Deutsch problem.

Classically, we need two calls to be made to the black box of $f(x)$ to get both $f(0)$ and $f(1)$ before we know if the function is constant or balanced. In a quantum setting, the same problem can be solved using just a single query to the oracle of $f(x)$ by using the Deutsch algorithm. Oracle of $f(x)$ is the function $U_F(x)$ that was discussed in the previous section.

The Deutsch algorithm is implemented as in the circuit in Fig. 2.4.

We will now compute the evolution of the state of the system.

$$|0\rangle |1\rangle \xrightarrow{H \otimes H} \frac{1}{\sqrt{2}}(|0\rangle + |1\rangle) |-\rangle$$

$$\xrightarrow{U_f} \frac{1}{\sqrt{2}}((-1)^{f(0)} |0\rangle + (-1)^{f(1)} |1\rangle) |-\rangle$$

$$\xrightarrow{H \otimes I} \frac{1}{2}\left[\left((-1)^{f(0)} + (-1)^{f(1)}\right) |0\rangle + \left((-1)^{f(0)} - (-1)^{f(1)}\right) |1\rangle\right] |-\rangle$$

Suppose we measure the final state of the system. We see that the probability of obtaining the state $|0\rangle$ is

$$Pr(|0\rangle) = \frac{1}{4}\left[(-1)^{f(0)} + (-1)^{f(1)}\right]^2$$

and that of obtaining $|1\rangle$ is

$$Pr(|1\rangle) = \frac{1}{4}\left[(-1)^{f(0)} - (-1)^{f(1)}\right]^2 = 1 - Pr(|0\rangle).$$

**Fig. 2.4** Quantum circuit for Deutsch algorithm

If the function $f(x)$ is balanced, then the probability of obtaining $|0\rangle$ vanishes to 0. Hence, we obtain only $|1\rangle$ upon measurement. On the other hand, if the function $f(x)$ is constant, then the probability of obtaining $|0\rangle$ equals 1 and so we obtain only $|0\rangle$ on measurement. So, with just a single call to the oracle $U_f$, we can conclude that the function is constant if the measurement outcome is $|0\rangle$ or is balanced if the measurement outcome is $|1\rangle$.

Even though the Deutsch algorithm is of limited practical use, it serves as a good tool to illustrate quantum parallelism and quantum interference. To determine if the function $f(x)$ is balanced or constant, we are actually not interested in the individual values of the function but in its global property $f(0) \oplus f(1)$. The Deutsch algorithm intelligently exploits this condition to obtain the solution using just a single query to the function.

## 2.5  The Deutsch-Jozsa Algorithm

The Deutsch-Jozsa algorithm is a natural extension of the Deutsch algorithm to $n$-bit Boolean functions. The Deutsch-Jozsa algorithm aims to solve the problem which is stated as follows: given an $n$-bit Boolean function $f(x)$ as an oracle, find if the function $f(x)$ is balanced or constant given the promise that $f(x)$ is either constant or balanced.

Before we describe the quantum algorithm, let us first analyze the classical complexity of solving this problem. An $n$-bit Boolean function $f(x)$ has $2^n$ output values, one for each $x \in \{0, 1\}^n$. We are given a promise that $f(x)$ is either constant or balanced. Recall that a balanced function has a truth-table with exactly $\frac{2^n}{2}$ zeros and $\frac{2^n}{2}$ ones. So, in the worst case, we will need $\frac{2^n}{2} + 1$ many queries to the function $f(x)$ so that if all the $\frac{2^n}{2} + 1$ $f(x)$ values are the same then we say that the function is constant, else we say that the function is balanced. The number of queries required in the worst case is exponential in $n$. Let us now see if Deutsch-Jozsa algorithm can provide us the solution in lesser number of queries to the function $f(x)$.

The quantum circuit of the Deutsch-Jozsa algorithm is shown in Fig. 2.5. The evolution of the state of the system is calculated below.

**Fig. 2.5** Quantum circuit for Deutsch-Jozsa algorithm

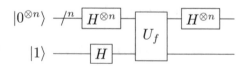

$$\left|0^{\otimes n}\right\rangle |1\rangle \xrightarrow{H^{\otimes n}\otimes H} \frac{1}{\sqrt{2^n}} \sum_x |x\rangle |-\rangle$$

$$\xrightarrow{U_f} \frac{1}{\sqrt{2^n}} \sum_x (-1)^{f(x)} |x\rangle |-\rangle$$

$$\xrightarrow{H^{\otimes n}\otimes I} \frac{1}{2^n} \sum_y \left[ \sum_x (-1)^{f(x)\oplus x\cdot y} \right] |y\rangle |-\rangle$$

where $x \cdot y$ denotes the bit-wise dot product $x_1 y_1 + x_2 y_2 + \cdots + x_n y_n$.

Now, upon observing the final state of the Deutsch-Jozsa algorithm, ignoring the last qubit, the probability of obtaining the state $\left|0^{\otimes n}\right\rangle$ is

$$Pr\left(\left|0^{\otimes n}\right\rangle\right) = \frac{1}{2^{2n}} \left[ \sum_{x\in\{0,1\}^n} (-1)^{f(x)} \right]^2. \tag{2.5}$$

We are promised that the function $f(x)$ is either balanced or constant. Let us first assume that the function is constant. Without loss of generality, let $f(x) = 1$ for all $x$. Then we have

$$Pr\left(\left|0^{\otimes n}\right\rangle\right) = \frac{1}{2^{2n}} \left[ \sum_{x\in\{0,1\}^n} (-1)^{f(x)} \right]^2 = \frac{1}{2^{2n}} \left[ \sum_{x\in\{0,1\}^n} -1 \right]^2 = \frac{1}{2^{2n}} \cdot 2^{2n} = 1.$$

So, a measurement would always yield the state $\left|0^{\otimes n}\right\rangle$ if the function $f(x)$ is constant.

Next, let us assume that the function $f(x)$ is balanced. Then, we have exactly $\frac{2^n}{2}$ points $x \in \{0, 1\}^n$ such that $f(x) = 0$ and exactly the same number of points such that $f(x) = 1$. Now, the probability of obtaining the state $\left|0^{\otimes n}\right\rangle$ becomes 0 since there would be exactly $\frac{2^n}{2}$ number of 1's and $\frac{2^n}{2}$ number of $-1$'s in the summation in Eq. 2.5. So, if the function $f(x)$ is balanced, then it is impossible to obtain the state $\left|0^{\otimes n}\right\rangle$ as the measurement outcome. Therefore, to summarize, $|0^n\rangle$ is always observed if $f(x)$ is constant and never observed if $f(x)$ is balanced.

Observe that the measurement outcomes obtained, in both the cases are mutually exclusive. Hence, the given function $f(x)$ can be characterized as balanced or as constant with just a single query to the oracle $U_f$. So, we obtain a quantum algorithm that is exponentially faster than the best known classical algorithm for distinguishing between a balanced and a constant Boolean function.

An interesting observation on the output of the algorithm is that the probability of obtaining a state $|a\rangle$ is

$$Pr(|a\rangle) = \frac{1}{2^{2n}} \left[ \sum_x (-1)^{f(x)\oplus x.a} \right]^2 = \left( \frac{W_f(a)}{2^n} \right)^2$$

which is the square of the normalized Walsh coefficient of the function $f(x)$ at the point $a$. We will discuss this in detail soon.

Let us now, implement the Deutsch-Jozsa algorithm in Qiskit. Let the given function be $f(x) = x_2 \oplus x_3 \oplus x_4$. The code is as follows:

```
1  #Importing classes and modules
2  from qiskit import *
3
4  #Building an oracle for the function f(x)=x2 xor x3
5  #xor x4.
6  #This is generally provided with the problem.
7  orcl = QuantumCircuit(5)
8  orcl.cx(1,4)
9  orcl.cx(2,4)
10 orcl.cx(3,4)
11 oracle = orcl.to_instruction()
12
13 #Creating quantum register, classical register
14 #and quantum circuit
15 q = QuantumRegister(5)
16 c = ClassicalRegister(4)
17 qc = QuantumCircuit(q,c)
18
19 #Implementing the Deutsch-Jozsa algorithm
20 qc.x(4)
21 qc.h(range(5))
22 qc.append(oracle,q)
23 qc.h(range(5))
24 for i in range(4):
25     qc.measure(q[i],c[3-i])
26
27 #Executing the code in the simulator
28 backend = Aer.get_backend('qasm_simulator')
29 qjob = execute(qc, backend, shots=1)
30 counts = qjob.result().get_counts()
31 print(counts)
```

**Listing 2.2**  Qiskit code for Deutsch-Jozsa algorithm

```
1  Output:
2  {'0111': 1}
```

In the code in Listing 2.2, in lines 7-11, we build an oracle that implements the function $f(x) = x_2 \oplus x_3 \oplus x_4$. In line 22, by using qc.append(oracle,q), we append the circuit of the oracle on the qubit register q to the circuit qc. In the output, we can see that the measurement outcome is $|0111\rangle$ which is not the state $|0000\rangle$. This implies that the function $f(x) = x_2 \oplus x_3 \oplus x_4$ is balanced.

## 2.6 The Bernstein-Vazirani Algorithm

Suppose that we are given a Boolean function $f(x)$ and we are also promised that the function $f(x)$ is linear, i.e., $f(x)$ can be written as $f(x) = a \cdot x$ for some $a \in \{0, 1\}^n$ where $a \cdot x = a_1 x_1 \oplus a_2 x_2 \oplus \cdots \oplus a_n x_n$. Say, the objective is to obtain the string $a$. This problem is called the Bernstein-Vazirani problem. Classically, this problem can be solved by obtaining the outputs of the function at all the $n$-bit strings of Hamming weight 1. This is because if $y(i)$ is the $n$-bit string of Hamming weight 1 such that 1 is in the $i^{th}$ position, then $f(y(i)) = a_i$ where $a_i$ is the $i^{th}$ bit of the string $a$. So classically, we would need to make $n$ queries to the black box of the function $f(x)$.

However, in a quantum setting, Bernstein-Vazirani algorithm solves this problem using a single query to the oracle of the function $f(x)$. The quantum circuit of the Bernstein-Vazirani algorithm is the same as that of the Deutsch-Jozsa algorithm (shown in Fig. 2.5). The final output state of the circuit after ignoring the last qubit is given as

$$|\psi_f\rangle = \frac{1}{2^n} \sum_y \left[ \sum_x (-1)^{f(x) \oplus x \cdot y} \right] |y\rangle .$$

Since we are given that $f(x) = a \cdot x$, for $y = a$ we have $f(x) \oplus x \cdot y = 0$ for all $x \in \{0, 1\}^n$. So, for $y = a$, we obtain

$$\sum_{x \in \{0,1\}^n} (-1)^{f(x) \oplus x \cdot y} = \sum_{x \in \{0,1\}^n} (-1)^0 = 2^n.$$

Therefore, on measuring the final state, the probability of obtaining the state $|a\rangle$ can be given as

$$Pr(|a\rangle) = \frac{1}{2^{2n}} \cdot (2^n)^2 = 1,$$

i.e., we obtain only $|a\rangle$ as the output using just a single query to the oracle of the function $f(x)$. Note that this algorithm would provide the same result if the function was $f(x) = (a \cdot x) \oplus 1$.

Let us now implement the Bernstein-Vazirani algorithm in Qiskit. Say, we are given the function $f(x) = x_1 \oplus x_2 \oplus x_3 \oplus x_4$ and a promise that $f(x)$ is a linear function. We find the string $a$ using the following code:

```
1  #Importing classes and modules
2  from qiskit import *
3
4  #Building an oracle for the function f(x)=x1 xor x2
5  #xor x3 xor x4
6  #This is generally provided with the problem.
7  orcl = QuantumCircuit(5)
8  orcl.cx(0,4)
9  orcl.cx(1,4)
10 orcl.cx(2,4)
11 orcl.cx(3,4)
```

```
12  oracle = orcl.to_instruction()
13
14  #Creating quantum register, classical register
15  #and quantum circuit
16  q = QuantumRegister(5)
17  c = ClassicalRegister(4)
18  qc = QuantumCircuit(q,c)
19
20  #Implementing the Deutsch-Jozsa algorithm
21  qc.h(4)
22  qc.h(range(5))
23  qc.append(oracle,q)
24  qc.h(range(5))
25  for i in range(4):
26      qc.measure(q[i],c[3-i])
27
28  #Executing the code in the simulator
29  backend = Aer.get_backend('qasm_simulator')
30  qjob = execute(qc, backend, shots=1)
31  counts = qjob.result().get_counts()
32  print(counts)
```

**Listing 2.3** Qiskit code for Bernstein-Vazirani algorithm

```
1  Output:
2  {'1111': 1}
```

From the output, we can see that the function $f(x)$ is the linear function of the form $f(x) = 1111 \cdot x$.

Notice that the Bernstein-Vazirani algorithm, even though using the same circuit as that of the Deutsch-Jozsa algorithm, looks at the same output state of the circuit from a different perspective than that of the Deutsch-Jozsa algorithm to solve a completely different problem.

## 2.7 Relation Between Deutsch-Jozsa and Walsh Spectrum

All the three algorithms above, essentially Deutsch-Jozsa in many forms, rely on the Walsh transform of a Boolean function. We saw in a previous section that given a Boolean function $f(x)$ as an oracle with a promise that $f(x)$ is either balanced or constant, the Deutsch-Jozsa algorithm determines if $f(x)$ is constant or balanced using one query. In fact, the Deutsch-Jozsa algorithm can be interpreted in terms of Walsh coefficients. Let us define an operator $\mathcal{D}_f$ in the following manner:

$$\mathcal{D}_f = (H^{\otimes n} \otimes I)U_f(H^{\otimes n} \otimes I),$$

The $U_f$ is the oracle of the function $f(x)$. Note that the operator $\mathcal{D}_f$ is the operator used in the Deutsch-Jozsa algorithm. We can see that

$$\mathcal{D}_f \left| 0^{\otimes n} \right\rangle \left| - \right\rangle = \frac{1}{2^n} \sum_{y \in \{0,1\}^n} \left[ \sum_{x \in \{0,1\}^n} (-1)^{f(x) \oplus (x \cdot y)} \right] \left| y \right\rangle \left| - \right\rangle = \left| \psi \right\rangle \left| - \right\rangle, \text{ (say)}.$$

Observe that the final state $\left| \psi \right\rangle$ can be rewritten in terms of the Walsh spectrum values as

$$\left| \psi \right\rangle = \sum_{y \in \{0,1\}^n} \frac{W_f(y)}{2^n} \left| y \right\rangle.$$

So, on measuring the final state $\left| \psi \right\rangle$, we obtain the measurement outcome as $\left| y \right\rangle$ with probability $\frac{W_f^2(y)}{2^{2n}}$. For the sake of brevity, let us define $\hat{f}(y)$ to be $\frac{W_f^2(y)}{2^{2n}}$.

Since the output of the measurement is probabilistic, we will be able to obtain the exact values of $\hat{f}(y)$ only if we run the algorithm infinitely many times. However, this is not feasible. So, in a quantum computer, instead of aiming to obtain the exact values of $\hat{f}(y)$ for all $y$'s, we estimate the values of $\hat{f}(y)$ allowing for some error. Even though this is a major drawback of computing Walsh spectrum in a quantum computer, for most of the applications good estimates of the Walsh spectral values are adequate.

As an example, let us take the 4-bit Boolean function $f(x) = x_1 x_2 \oplus x_3 \oplus x_4$. Computing the Walsh spectrum of $f(x)$ is quite straightforward in a classical computer, e.g, by using the following Python code:

```python
#Defining a function that outputs (x1*x2) xor x3
#xor x4
def func(x):
    x_arr = [0]*4
    for i in range(4):
        x_arr[3-i] = x%2
        x = (x-x_arr[3-i])/2
    return ((x_arr[0]*x_arr[1])+x_arr[2]+x_arr[3])%2


#Defining a function that output the dot product of
#bit strings of x and y
def dot(x,y):
    x_arr = [0]*4
    y_arr = [0]*4
    dot = 0
    for i in range(4):
        x_arr[3-i] = x%2
        x = (x-x_arr[3-i])/2
        y_arr[3-i] = y%2
        y = (y-y_arr[3-i])/2
        dot = dot + (x_arr[3-i]*y_arr[3-i])
    return dot%2


#Calculating the Walsh coefficients of the above
#function at all points
w_f = [0]*16
```

```
29 for y in range(16):
30     for x in range(16):
31         w_f[y] = w_f[y] + ((-1)**func(x))*((-1)**dot(x
       ,y))
32
33 for i in range(16):
34     print(bin(i)[2:].zfill(4), ":", w_f[i], end=', ')
```
**Listing 2.4** Python code for Walsh spectrum

```
1 Output:
2 0000 : 0.0, 0001 : 0.0, 0010 : 0.0, 0011 : 8.0, 0100 :
      0.0, 0101 : 0.0, 0110 : 0.0, 0111 : 8.0, 1000 :
      0.0, 1001 : 0.0, 1010 : 0.0, 1011 : 8.0, 1100 :
      0.0, 1101 : 0.0, 1110 : 0.0, 1111 : -8.0,
```

We can see from the output that the Walsh coefficient at the points 0011, 0111, 1011 are 8 and that at the point 1111 is -8. At the rest of the points, the Walsh coefficient is 0.

For implementing the Deutsch-Jozsa algorithm to estimate the Walsh spectrum of the function $f(x)$, the code is given in Listing 2.5.

```
1 #Importing the required classes and modules
2 from qiskit import *
3
4 #Building an oracle for the function f(x)=x1x2+x3+x4.
5 orcl = QuantumCircuit(5)
6 orcl.ccx(0,1,4)
7 orcl.cx(2,4)
8 orcl.cx(3,4)
9 oracle = orcl.to_instruction()
10
11 #Creating quantum register, classical register
12 #and quantum circuit
13 q = QuantumRegister(5)
14 c = ClassicalRegister(4)
15 qc = QuantumCircuit(q,c)
16
17 #Implementing the circuit of Deutsch-Jozsa algorithm.
18 qc.x(q[4])
19 for i in range(5):
20     qc.h(q[i])
21 qc.append(oracle,q)
22 for i in range(5):
23     qc.h(q[i])
24 for i in range(4):
25     qc.measure(q[3-i],c[i])
```
**Listing 2.5** Circuit for obtaining walsh spectrum using the Deutsch-Jozsa algorithm

To understand how the number of shots affect the estimation, we execute the circuit three times; first using 100 shots, then using 1000 shots and finally with 8000 shots. The executions are performed in a quantum simulator using the following code:

```
1  #Executing the circuit in simulator
2  backend = Aer.get_backend('qasm_simulator')
3  qjob_sim_100 = execute(qc, backend, shots=100)
4  counts_sim_100 = qjob_sim_100.result().get_counts()
5  qjob_sim_1000 = execute(qc, backend, shots=1000)
6  counts_sim_1000 = qjob_sim_1000.result().get_counts()
7  qjob_sim_8000 = execute(qc, backend, shots=8000)
8  counts_sim_8000 = qjob_sim_8000.result().get_counts()
9
10 for count1, count2, count3 in zip(counts_sim_100,
       counts_sim_1000, counts_sim_8000):
11     counts_sim_100[count1] /= 100
12     counts_sim_1000[count2] /= 1000
13     counts_sim_8000[count3] /= 8000
14
15 print("Estimate of Walsh spectrum using 100 shots : \n
       ",counts_sim_100,"\n")
16 print("Estimate of Walsh spectrum using 1000 shots : \
       n",counts_sim_1000,"\n")
17 print("Estimate of Walsh spectrum using 8000 shots : \
       n",counts_sim_8000,"\n")
```

**Listing 2.6**  Executing the circuit created in Listing 2.5 on a simulator with varied number of shots.

```
1  Output:
2  Estimate of Walsh spectrum using 100 shots :
3   {'1011': 0.25, '0011': 0.29, '1111': 0.2, '0111':
       0.26}
4
5  Estimate of Walsh spectrum using 1000 shots :
6   {'1011': 0.236, '0011': 0.259, '1111': 0.248, '0111':
       0.257}
7
8  Estimate of Walsh spectrum using 8000 shots :
9   {'1011': 0.242875, '0011': 0.254625, '1111':
       0.257625, '0111': 0.244875}
```

In the output of Listing 2.6, for points not in the returned set of values, the $\hat{f}(y)$ at those points should be inferred as 0. From the output of Listing 2.4, we can deduce that the square of the normalized Walsh coefficient $\hat{f}(y)$ at the points $y \in \{0011, 0111, 1011, 1111\}$ is $\frac{64}{256} = 0.25$.

First observe that the values that we obtained when using shots=100 are very rough estimates of the Walsh spectral values since we can see that the estimate of $\hat{f}(y)$ at points 0011 and 1111 were returned as 0.29 and 0.2 respectively, which are relatively far from the expected value of 0.25. In the estimates returned by using 1000 shots, we can see that they are better than those obtained using 100 shots, but still worse than those obtained using 8000 shots. Naturally, the best of the three estimates were obtained when we used 8000 shots. So, we can witness that the accuracy of the estimates increases with the increase in the number of shots used.

Next, we implement the circuit in Listing 2.5 on an actual quantum computer. For this we use the 5-qubit machine *ibmq_belem*. The execution is done using the following code:

```
1 #Obtaining the IBMQ provider and backend.
2 IBMQ.load_account()
3 provider = IBMQ.get_provider()
4 backend = provider.get_backend('ibmq_belem')
5
6 #Executing the circuit on ibmqx2
7 qjob_real = execute(qc, backend, shots=1000)
8 counts_real = qjob_real.result().get_counts()
9 for count in counts_real:
10    counts_real[count] /= 1000
11 print("Estimate of Walsh spectrum using 1000 shots on
       ibmq_belem : \n", counts_real, "\n")
```

**Listing 2.7** Executing the circuit created in Listing 2.5 on *ibmq_belem* with 1000 shots.

```
1 Output:
2 Estimate of Walsh spectrum using 1000 shots on
     ibmq_belem:
3  {'1110': 0.031, '0011': 0.143, '1010': 0.01, '1111':
      0.188, '1101': 0.066, '0010': 0.019, '0110': 0.021,
      '0101': 0.07, '0111': 0.184, '1011': 0.091,
      '1000': 0.013, '0100': 0.029, '1100': 0.014,
      '0001': 0.056, '0000': 0.036, '1001': 0.029}
```

We can observe in the output that the estimates of $\hat{f}(y)$ is non-zero for all $y \in \{0, 1\}^n$. It can also be observed that the errors in the estimates are very high. A visual comparison between the estimates obtained using the simulator and that using the real backend, both with 1000 shots, can be obtained using the following code snippet.

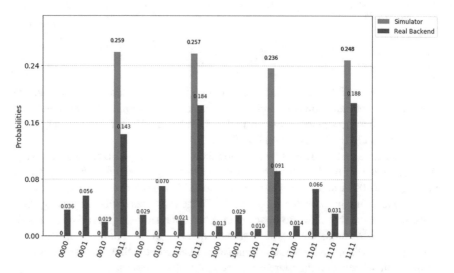

**Fig. 2.6** Comparison between the estimates obtained using simulator and real backend

```
1 #Importing the visualization tool.
2 from qiskit.tools.visualization import plot_histogram
3 plot_histogram([count_sim_1000, counts_real], legend=[
     "Simulator", "Real Backend"])
```
**Listing 2.8**  Code to compare the estimates obtained using a simulator and a real backend.

The histogram obtained for these results is shown in Fig. 2.6.

From Fig. 2.6, we can clearly see that the estimates obtained from the real backend are very much error prone. These errors are mostly attributed to the de-coherence of the quantum system and the undesired interactions with the environment. Detailed discussion on this is out of the scope of this book.

# Further Reading

Boolean functions and their cryptographic properties received lot of attention in research literature. For a comprehensive idea about cryptographically significant Boolean functions, one may refer to [2]. For more about the different properties and Walsh spectrum of Boolean functions, one may refer to [7–10].

One of the most celebrated quantum algorithms is Deutsch-Jozsa [4]. This can deterministically distinguish a balanced and a constant Boolean function with linear resource and in constant time complexity. This is more efficient than any algorithm available in the classical domain. Most interestingly, this algorithm outputs (before the measurement) a multi-qubit state which is a superposition of the basis states with their corresponding amplitudes proportional to the Walsh spectrum values. This can be exploited in many other applications as we will see in the following chapter. A simpler version of Deutsch-Jozsa [4] appeared earlier, which is referred to as Deutsch algorithm [3]. This is a special case where the given function is an 1-bit Boolean function. The Bernstein-Vazirani Algorithm [1] can also be considered as another special case, when the function under inspection is affine, i.e., the Walsh spectrum mass is only at a single point, and everywhere else it is zero.

Other different combinatorial properties can be studied by simple modifications of Deutsch-Jozsa algorithm [4]. For example the Nega-Hadamard transform has been studied in [5]. For advanced algebraic and combinatorial properties one may have a look at [6] and try to explore efficient quantum algorithms in these directions. Further, in the following chapters we will see that the quantum output of Deutsch-Jozsa algorithm (before the measurement) can be exploited to explore several other cryptographic properties such as resiliency. That is, the Deutsch-Jozsa algorithm is not only a celebrated algorithm, but it provides several other directions in further analysis of Boolean functions.

# References

1. Bernstein, E., Vazirani, U.: Quantum complexity theory. In: Proceedings of the 25th Annual ACM Symposium on Theory of Computing, pp. 11–20. ACM Press, New York (1993)
2. Cusick, T., Stănică, P.: Cryptographic Boolean Functions and Applications, 2nd edn. Academic, New York (2017)
3. Deutsch, D.: Quantum computational networks. Proc. R. Soc. Lond., Ser. A **425**, 73 (1989)
4. Deutsch, D., Jozsa, R.: Rapid solution of problems by quantum computation. Proc. R. Soc. Lond. **A439**, 553–558 (1992)
5. Gangopadhyay, S., Maitra, S., Sinha, N., Stănică, P.: Quantum algorithms related HN-transforms of Boolean functions. C2SI 2017, 314-327
6. Jothishwaran, C.A., Tkachenko, A., Gangopadhyay, S., Riera, C., Stănică, P.: A quantum algorithm to estimate the Gowers U2 norm and linearity testing of Boolean functions. Quantum Inf. Proc. **19**(9), 311 (2020)
7. MacWillams, F.J., Sloane, N.J.A.: The Theory of Error Correcting Codes. North Holland (1977)
8. Siegenthaler, T.: Correlation-immunity of nonlinear combining functions for cryptographic applications. IEEE Trans. Inf. Theory, IT- **30**(5), 776–780 (1984). September
9. Sarkar, P., Maitra, S.: Nonlinearity bounds and constructions of resilient Boolean functions. In: Advances in Cryptology - CRYPTO 2000. Lecture Notes in Computer Science, vol. 1880, pp. 515–532. Springer, Berlin (2000)
10. Guo-Zhen, X., Massey, J.: A spectral characterization of correlation immune combining functions. IEEE Trans. Inf. Theory **34**(3), 569–571 (1988). May

# Chapter 3
# Grover's Algorithm and Walsh Spectrum

**Abstract**  Grover's algorithm provides a square root improvement over its classical counterpart in searching an unsorted array. The most important part of this algorithm is that, it can amplify the amplitude of a subset of states and reduce that of the others. First, we show how the satisfying inputs of a Boolean function can be efficiently discovered by the Grover's strategy. Further, one can consider the state out of the Deutsch-Jozsa algorithm that is related to Walsh spectrum of a Boolean function, and then try to amplify certain places through Grover to understand the Walsh spectrum distribution with further accuracy. In particular, we provide detailed understanding of how the nonlinearity and resiliency of a Boolean function can be studied in this direction. Examples and Qiskit codes are presented here to explain the idea with complete details.

**Keywords**  Boolean functions · Bernstein-Vazirani algorithm · Deutsch-Jozsa algorithm · Grover's algorithm · Walsh transform

## 3.1  Grover's Algorithm

Grover's algorithm is one of the most popular quantum algorithms that is used for searching an element in an unsorted array. Searching an element of interest among $N$ elements is one of the basic tasks in computer science. When the elements are not sorted and there is no additional data structure, e.g., a binary search tree, the best known classical algorithm must query all the $N$ elements in the worst case. Surprisingly, Grover's algorithm can find the element in just $O(\sqrt{N})$ queries. This polynomial speedup may look pale against the algorithms presented in the previous chapter which promised exponential speedups over the classical algorithms, but Grover's algorithm is extraordinary and noteworthy due to the ubiquity of the search problem that it solves. Today, it is the most common subroutine in the hundreds of quantum algorithms that exist for various types of problems.

© The Author(s), under exclusive license to Springer Nature Singapore Pte Ltd. 2021      59
T. SAPV et al., *Quantum Algorithms for Cryptographically Significant Boolean Functions*,
SpringerBriefs in Computer Science,
https://doi.org/10.1007/978-981-16-3061-3_3

The most important element in this algorithm is a small block of code called the Grover's iterate. It implements the following operator.

$$G = H^{\otimes n} U_{\bar{0}} H^{\otimes n} U_f.$$

In this operator, $H^{\otimes n}$ is the Hadamard operator on $n$ qubits, $U_f$ is the oracle that marks the element of interest and $U_{\bar{0}}$ is the operator that flips the phase of all the basis states except the $|0\rangle^{\otimes n}$ state.

The action of $U_{\bar{0}}$ on the standard basis states can be expressed as

$$U_{\bar{0}} |x\rangle = \left\{ \begin{array}{l} -|x\rangle \text{ if } x \neq 0^n \\ |x\rangle \text{ if } x = 0^n \end{array} \right\} = 2 |0^{\otimes n}\rangle \langle 0^{\otimes n}| - I.$$

The last expression is possible due to the completeness relation discussed in Sect. 1.6.

We can rewrite the Grover's iterate after expanding $U_{\bar{0}}$ as a product of two operators. In this new expression for $G$, we use $|S\rangle$ to denote the equal superposition of all the $N$ states corresponding to the $N$ items.

$$G = H^{\otimes n} (2 |0\rangle \langle 0| - I) H^{\otimes n} U_f = (2 |S\rangle \langle S| - I) U_f.$$

Let us first examine the functioning of $U_f$. We know that the operator $U_f$ marks the *good* state, i.e., $U_f$ acts as

$$U_f(\alpha |bad\rangle + \beta |good\rangle) \longrightarrow \alpha |bad\rangle - \beta |good\rangle.$$

This is essentially a reflection about the *bad* state. Next, consider the operator $2 |S\rangle \langle S| - I$. To understand its behaviour, denote by $|S^{\perp}\rangle$ a state that is orthogonal to $|S\rangle$ and apply $2 |S\rangle \langle S| - I$ on any state that is a superposition of the two orthogonal states $|S\rangle$ and $|S^{\perp}\rangle$. We will see below that the operator performs a reflection of this state about the state $|S\rangle$.

$$\left(2 |S\rangle \langle S| - I\right)\left(\alpha |S\rangle + \beta |S^{\perp}\rangle\right)$$
$$= \alpha\left(2 |S\rangle \langle S| S\rangle - |S\rangle\right) + \beta\left(2 |S\rangle \langle S| S^{\perp}\rangle - |S^{\perp}\rangle\right)$$
$$= \alpha\left(2 |S\rangle - |S\rangle\right) + \beta\left(0 - |S^{\perp}\rangle\right)$$
$$= \alpha |S\rangle - \beta |S^{\perp}\rangle.$$

Grover's algorithm starts by preparing an equal superposition of $N$ states corresponding to all the $N$ items of the list. The Grover's iterate is then applied on this superposition, $\sqrt{N}$ number of times. The final state is then measured; it is known that the observed state represents the item of interest with high probability. A circuit for the Grover's algorithm can be seen in Fig. 3.1.

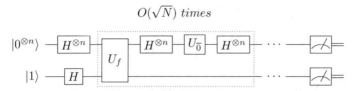

**Fig. 3.1** Quantum circuit for Grover's algorithm

To understand the working of the algorithm, consider the following generic example. Let us assume for example we have a list of $N = 2^n$ number of items of which we are interested in finding a particular element. We call the element of interest *good* and the rest of the elements *bad*. Then, a state containing the equal super position of all the $N$ elements is of the form

$$|\psi\rangle = \frac{1}{\sqrt{N}} |good\rangle + \sqrt{\frac{N-1}{N}} |bad\rangle .$$

We can see that the probability of obtaining the *good* state on measuring $|\psi\rangle$ is $\frac{1}{N}$. Choose $\theta$ from $[0, \frac{\pi}{2}]$ such that $\sin \theta = \left(\frac{1}{\sqrt{N}}\right)$. Then we have

$$|\psi\rangle = \sin \theta \, |good\rangle + \cos \theta \, |bad\rangle .$$

Notice that the angle $\theta$ is the angle formed by the state $|\psi\rangle$ with the state $|bad\rangle$[1]. On applying $U_f$, we obtain the state

$$\left|\psi'\right\rangle = -\sin \theta \, |good\rangle + \cos \theta \, |bad\rangle .$$

Now, we know that

$$|S\rangle = \sum_{x \in \{0,1\}^n} |x\rangle = \frac{1}{\sqrt{N}} |good\rangle + \sqrt{\frac{N-1}{N}} |bad\rangle = \sin \theta \, |good\rangle + \cos \theta \, |bad\rangle .$$

Notice that, $|S\rangle$ and $|\psi\rangle$ essentially represent the same state. Thus, the state $\left|S^{\perp}\right\rangle$ can be given as

$$\left|S^{\perp}\right\rangle = \cos \theta \, |good\rangle - \sin \theta \, |bad\rangle .$$

Observe that

---

[1] The concept of angle will be better understood during the discussion on the geometric interpretation of Grover's algorithm provided below.

$$\langle S| \, S^{\perp}\rangle = \Big( \sin\theta \, \langle good| + \cos\theta \, \langle bad| \, \Big)\Big( \cos\theta \, |good\rangle - \sin\theta \, |bad\rangle \Big)$$
$$= \cos\theta \sin\theta - \cos\theta \sin\theta = 0$$

and

$$|S\rangle \, \langle S| + |S^{\perp}\rangle\langle s^{\perp}| = |good\rangle \, \langle good| + |bad\rangle \, \langle bad| = I.$$

Hence, $|S\rangle$ and $|S^{\perp}\rangle$ form a basis. This allows us to write $|\psi'\rangle$ as a superposition of $|S\rangle$ and $|S'\rangle$ as in the following form.

$$|\psi'\rangle = - \sin\theta \, |good\rangle + \cos\theta \, |bad\rangle$$
$$= \sin(\theta - 2\theta) \, |good\rangle + \cos(2\theta - \theta) \, |bad\rangle$$
$$= \Big( \cos 2\theta \sin\theta - \sin 2\theta \cos\theta \Big) \, |good\rangle + \Big( \cos 2\theta \cos\theta + \sin 2\theta \sin\theta \Big) \, |bad\rangle$$
$$= \cos 2\theta \Big( \sin\theta \, |good\rangle + \cos\theta \, |bad\rangle \Big) - \sin 2\theta \Big( \cos\theta \, |good\rangle - \sin\theta \, |bad\rangle \Big)$$
$$= \cos 2\theta \, |S\rangle - \sin 2\theta \, |S^{\perp}\rangle.$$

Now, applying the operator $2 \, |S\rangle \, \langle S| - I$ on $|\psi'\rangle$ we have

$$|\psi''\rangle = \Big( 2 \, |S\rangle \, \langle S| - I \Big) |\psi'\rangle$$
$$= \Big( 2 \, |S\rangle \, \langle S| - I \Big)\Big( \cos 2\theta \, |S\rangle - \sin 2\theta \, |S^{\perp}\rangle \Big)$$
$$= 2 \cos 2\theta \, |S\rangle \, \langle S| \, S\rangle - \cos 2\theta \, |S\rangle - 2 \sin 2\theta \, |S\rangle \, \langle S| \, S^{\perp}\rangle + \sin 2\theta \, |S^{\perp}\rangle$$
$$= \cos 2\theta \, |S\rangle + \sin 2\theta \, |S^{\perp}\rangle.$$

Then, $|\psi''\rangle$ in terms of the $|good\rangle$ and $|bad\rangle$ states can be given as

$$|\psi''\rangle = \cos 2\theta \, |S\rangle + \sin 2\theta \, |S^{\perp}\rangle$$
$$= \cos 2\theta \Big( \sin\theta \, |good\rangle + \cos\theta \, |bad\rangle \Big) + \sin 2\theta \Big( \cos\theta \, |good\rangle - \sin\theta \, |bad\rangle \Big)$$
$$= \sin 3\theta \, |good\rangle + \cos 3\theta \, |bad\rangle .$$

If the state $|\psi''\rangle$ is measured, we would observe the state $|good\rangle$ with probability $\sin^2 3\theta$. Thus, a single application of $G$ can increase the probability of observing a good state from $\sin^2 \theta$ to $\sin^2 3\theta$. The above calculation can be extended to show that $k$ applications of $G$ can increase the probability of observing a good state to $\sin^2 (2k + 1)\theta$.

### 3.1.1 Geometric Interpretation of Grover's Algorithm

We saw above that every application of the Grover's iterate can be perceived as a sequence of two reflections. Let us now see this in action using the help of geometry. Imagine a two dimensional plane spanned by the states $|good\rangle$ and $|bad\rangle$ with real amplitudes. An arbitrary state $|\psi\rangle = \sin\theta\,|good\rangle + \cos\theta\,|bad\rangle$ belongs to this plane as illustrated in Fig. 3.2a. For simplicity we assume that $\theta \in [0, \pi/2]$. We can observe that the state $|\psi\rangle$ forms angles $\theta$ and $\frac{\pi}{2} - \theta$ with the states $|bad\rangle$ and $|good\rangle$, respectively.

Applying the operator $U_f$ on $|\psi\rangle$, the state $|\psi\rangle$ reflects about $|bad\rangle$ to form the state $\left|\psi'\right\rangle = U_f\,|\psi\rangle$. However, the state $\left|\psi'\right\rangle$ still forms an angle $\theta$ with $|bad\rangle$ and an angle of $2\theta$ with the state $|\psi\rangle$ as shown in Fig. 3.2b. Next, applying the operator $\left(2\,|S\rangle\,\langle S| - I\right)$ on $\left|\psi'\right\rangle$ reflects the state $\left|\psi'\right\rangle$ about the state $|S\rangle$. Note that the state $|S\rangle$ is same as the state $|\psi\rangle$. So, on reflection about the state $|S\rangle$, the final state $\left|\psi''\right\rangle = U_{Ref_s}U_f\,|\psi\rangle$ ends up as in Fig. 3.2c where the angle made by $\left|\psi''\right\rangle$ with the state $|\psi\rangle$ remains equal but in the other direction. Therefore, the state $\left|\psi''\right\rangle$ makes an

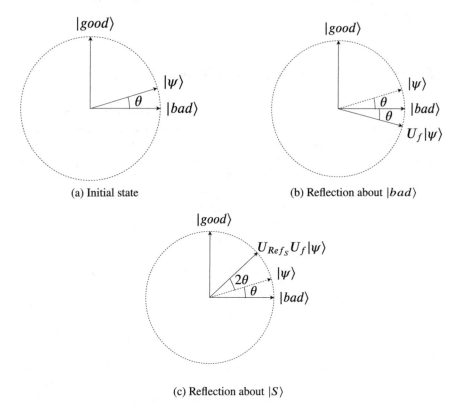

(a) Initial state      (b) Reflection about $|bad\rangle$

(c) Reflection about $|S\rangle$

**Fig. 3.2** Grover's iteration as reflections

angle of $3\theta$ with the state $|bad\rangle$, that is, moves far from $|bad\rangle$. Hence, on applying the Grover's iterate once, we have the state

$$|\psi''\rangle = \sin 3\theta \,|good\rangle + \cos 3\theta \,|bad\rangle \,.$$

Note that the state gained an angle of $2\theta$ with one iteration of Grover's iterate. Similarly, after the second iteration the state gains an angle of $2\theta$ forming the resultant state $|\phi\rangle = \sin 5\theta \,|good\rangle + \cos 5\theta \,|bad\rangle$. Hence, after $k$ many applications of Grover's iterate, the angle formed by the resultant state with the state $|bad\rangle$ is $(2k + 1)\theta$. To obtain the *good* state with probability 1, we can see that we need to perform $k$ iterations of Grover's iterate such that $(2k + 1)\theta$ is equal to $\frac{\pi}{2}$. However, the equality is not possible for all $\theta$ since the increase of angle is discrete. So we settle for a $k$ such that $(2k + 1)\theta$ is as close as possible to $\frac{\pi}{2}$; this allows us to obtain $|good\rangle$ with a "high" probability after measurement. Mathematically, the optimal $k$ can be expressed as $\left\lceil \frac{\pi}{4\theta} - \frac{1}{2} \right\rceil = O(\sqrt{N})$ using elementary trigonometry.

In the generic example, we assume that we have a single item of interest in the list of $N$ items. This can be extended to cases where there are some $t$ number of items of interest. For such a case it can be shown that the optimal number of iterations required is $O(\sqrt{N/t})$.

## 3.2  Finding Satisfying Inputs of a Boolean Function

It should be clear by now that Grover's algorithm has a simple yet powerful promise. It can search among a group of elements at a rate that is quadratically faster compared to that of the classical algorithms that performs a linear scan. The algorithm also composes nicely, meaning, it can be used in a black-box manner in any algorithm where some kind of searching is involved. This tempting property has led to this algorithm finding its way in a multitude of applications from several domains.

Therefore, it should not appear as a surprise that the application of Grover's algorithm in the field of analysis of Boolean function is very wide. For instance, imagine that we are provided with an $n$-bit Boolean function $f(x)$ and the information that $f(x) = f(y)$ for exactly one pair of $x, y$. Without any additional information and additional data structures, any classical algorithm in the worst case would need to check all the $(2^n \times 2^n)/2$ pairs of strings before it discovers the colliding pairs. However, we can use Grover's algorithm to find the pair by making only $O(2^n)$ queries to $f(x)$. There exist better quantum algorithms for this specific problem but the example illustrates the simple manner in which we can incorporate Grover's algorithm for our applications.

We now demonstrate the implementation of Grover's algorithm in Qiskit. Our objective is to find the input point $x$ for which the 4-bit Boolean function $f(x) = x_2x_3 \oplus x_1x_2x_3 \oplus x_2x_3x_4 \oplus x_1x_2x_3x_4$ outputs 1. This is performed in the following code.

```
1 #Importing the required classes and modules
2 from qiskit import *
3 from qiskit.circuit.library import *
4
5 #Building an oracle for the function
6 #f(x)=x2x3+x1x2x3+x2x3x4+x1x2x3x4
7 #This is the U_f.
8 def oracle():
9     orcl = QuantumCircuit(4)
10    orcl.x(3)
11    orcl.append(ZGate().control(3,ctrl_state='110'),
       range(4))
12    orcl.x(3)
13    return orcl
14
15 #Number of Grover iterations to be implemented
16 num_iter = 3
17
18 #Creating quantum register, classical register
19 #and quantum circuit
20 q = QuantumRegister(4)
21 c = ClassicalRegister(4)
22 qc = QuantumCircuit(q,c)
23
24 #Initializing the initial state to equal superposition
25 qc.h(range(4))
26
27 #Implementing Grover's iteration for num_iter
28 #many iterations
29 for k in range(num_iter):
30    qc.append(oracle(), range(4))
31    qc.h(range(4))
32    qc.x(3)
33    qc.append(ZGate().control(3,ctrl_state='000'),
       range(4))
34    qc.x(3)
35    qc.h(range(4))
36
37 #Measuring the qubits
38 for i in range(4):
39    qc.measure(i,3-i)
40
41 #Executing the circuit in simulator
42 backend = Aer.get_backend('qasm_simulator')
43 qjob = execute(qc, backend, shots=100)
44 counts = qjob.result().get_counts()
45 print(counts)
```

**Listing 3.1** Qiskit code for implementing Grover's algorithm

```
1 Output:
2 {'0000': 1, '0110': 96, '0111': 1, '1000': 1, '1110':
    1}
```

In Listing 3.1, the function `oracle()` returns the oracle for the given function $f(x)$. Even though we construct the oracle for the function $f(x)$ in our code, we are generally provided the oracle of the function with the problem. Since $f(x)$ is a 4-bit Boolean function, the size of its truth table is $2^4 = 16$. So it is expected that the Grover's iterate is applied a total of $num\_iter \approx \sqrt{16} = 4$ many times. But you will be able to notice that the amplitude of the state $|0110\rangle$ attains the maximum when $num\_iter = 3$. You can verify this by changing the value of $num\_iter$ and we encourage you to do this. Notice that the reflection about the state $|0000\rangle$ is easily performed by flipping the last qubit $q_4$, applying the control `ZGate()` controlled on the first three qubits being 0 and the target being $q_4$ and then flipping $q_4$ back. This can be seen in line 33 of Listing 3.1.

In the output, we can observe that on measurement, the state that is observed with a high probability is $|0110\rangle$. It can be easily verified that $f(0110) = 1$.

## 3.3 Nonlinearity

In the previous chapter, we investigated the Walsh spectrum of a Boolean function. One of the prime cryptographic measures on Boolean functions are their nonlinearity. We will first discuss the connection between the nonlinearity of a Boolean function and its Walsh spectrum and then describe how to measure nonlinearity using a quantum computer.

The nonlinearity of an $n$-bit Boolean function $f(x)$ is defined as the minimum Hamming distance from the function to the set of *all affine* Boolean functions. Mathematically,

$$\eta(f) = \min_{a,b} \frac{dist(f, \chi'_{a,b})}{2^n}$$

where $\chi'_{a,b} = a \cdot x \oplus b$ in which $a \cdot x = a_1 \cdot x_1 \oplus a_2 \cdot x_2 \oplus \ldots \oplus a_n \cdot x_n$ and $a_i, b \in \{0, 1\}$. The set $\{\chi'_{a,b} : a \in \{0, 1\}^n, b \in \{0, 1\}\}$ is the set of all affine Boolean functions. Recall that the Hamming distance between two Boolean functions $f(x)$ and $g(x)$ is the number of points $a$ such that $f(a) \neq g(a)$. Then, we can write the Walsh coefficient of a function $f(x)$ at the point $a$ as

$$\hat{f}(a) = 1 - 2\frac{dist(f, \chi'_{a,0})}{2^n} = 2\frac{dist(f, \chi'_{a,1})}{2^n} - 1.$$

This implies that $\frac{dist(f, \chi'_{a,0})}{2^n} = \frac{1}{2}(1 - \hat{f}(a))$ and $\frac{dist(f, \chi'_{a,1})}{2^n} = \frac{1}{2}(1 + \hat{f}(a))$. Using these forms we can rewrite $\eta(f)$ as

$$\eta(f) = \min_a \left(\frac{1}{2}(1 - |\hat{f}(a)|)\right) = \frac{1}{2} - \frac{1}{2}\max_a\left(|\hat{f}(a)|\right).$$

Let $\hat{f}_{\max} = \max_a\{|\hat{f}(a)|\}$. We know that $|\hat{f}_{\max}| \leq 1$ where the equality holds for affine functions and $|\hat{f}_{\max}| \geq \frac{1}{\sqrt{2^n}}$ where the equality hold for bent functions. As a consequence, we have the bounds of the nonlinearity of a Boolean function as

$$0 \leq \eta(f) \leq \frac{1}{2} - \frac{1}{2} \cdot \frac{1}{2^{n/2}}.$$

Let us now look at the computational cost of exactly computing the nonlinearity of a Boolean function given as oracle. It is quite evident that we would need at least exponential calls to the oracle since we need to find the distance of the given function from all the $2^n$ possible linear functions. So a naive computation of nonlinearity would require us to query the oracle about $O(2^{2n})$ times. We arrive at this value by querying the oracle $2^n$ times to find the distance of the given function from one particular linear function and making that many queries for all $2^n$ linear functions. We can perform better if we exploit the form of nonlinearity in terms of Walsh spectrum, since the Walsh spectrum at all $2^n$ points can be computed with $\Theta(n2^n)$ queries using the Fast Hadamard transform (similar to Fast Fourier transform). In fact this is the best possible classical algorithm to compute the exact nonlinearity of a given Boolean function.

The implementation of the naive algorithm to compute the exact nonlinearity can be done using the following Python code:

```
#Importing the required packages
import numpy as np
import scipy
from scipy.linalg import hadamard

#Defining a function that returns the function values
#as an array.
def func_arr():
    func = []
    for i in range(16):
        x = bin(i)[2:].zfill(4)
        f = (int(x[0])*int(x[1]))+(int(x[1])*int(x[3])
        func.append((-1)**(f%2))
    return func

#Defining a function that on providing an array of
#function values as input, it exactly computes and
#returns the maximum of the absolute values of the
#Walsh coefficients of the given function.
def fhat_max(func):
    h = scipy.linalg.hadamard(len(func))
    fhat = np.dot(h,func)
    f_abs = []
    for i in range(len(func)):
        f_abs.append(abs(fhat[i]))
    return max(f_abs)/16
```

```
28 nl = (1/2)-(fhat_max(func_arr())/2)
29 print('The nonlinearity of the function f(x)= x1x2+
      x3x4 is : ', nl)
```

**Listing 3.2** Python code for computing the nonlinearity of the function $x_1x_2 \oplus x_3x_4$

```
1 Output:
2 The nonlinearity of the function f(x)= x1x2+x3x4 is :
      0.375
```

The python code for computing the exact nonlinearity is quite straight forward. We define two functions, `func_arr()` and `fhat_max()`. `func_arr()` returns an array such that the $i^{th}$ element of the array is $f(i_{bin})$ where $i_{bin}$ is the binary representation of $i$. `fhat_max()` takes as input an array that contains the $f(i_{bin})$ as the $i^{th}$ element and returns the maximum of the $|\hat{f}(x)|$s by simply calculating $|\hat{f}(x)|$ for each $x$ deterministically and obtaining the maximum over all input $x$.

As we can see, the nonlinearity of the function $f(x) = x_1x_2 \oplus x_3x_4$ is 0.375. It is easy to observe that computing the exact nonlinearity as in Listing 3.2 requires $O(2^{2n})$ many queries to the oracle, if the function was given as an oracle (which is generally the case). Alternatively, we can use methods involving Fast Fourier transform that uses $2^n$ space and computes the exact nonlinearity in just $O(n \cdot 2^n)$ oracle queries.

However, for most applications it is sufficient to obtain an estimate of the nonlinearity instead of computing the exact nonlinearity of the functions. It is expected for the computational cost of estimation to depend directly on the required accuracy. At the moment of writing the book we are not aware of any quantum algorithm that estimates the nonlinearity of a Boolean function in better than exponential time for any given accuracy.

## 3.4 Linearity Testing

We learnt about nonlinearity in the previous section but we did not come across any quantum algorithm for the same. A related, simpler problem for which there is a quantum algorithm is that of detecting if a function $f(x)$ is linear (i.e., has zero nonlinearity) or not.

We saw previously that an $n$-bit linear function $f_l(x)$ can be represented as $f_l(x) = a \cdot x$ for some $a \in \{0, 1\}^n$. Alternatively, a Boolean function $f(x)$ is said to be a linear function if $f(x) \oplus f(y) = f(x \oplus y)$ for all $x, y \in \{0, 1\}^n$. The equivalence of the two definitions is quite straight forward. If a function $f(x)$ is defined as $f(x) = a \cdot x$, then for any two $n$-bit strings $x$ and $y$, we have $f(x \oplus y) = a \cdot (x \oplus y) = (a \cdot x) \oplus (a \cdot y) = f(x) \oplus f(y)$. The proof of the converse is left to the readers as an exercise.

Given two functions $f$ and $g$, we say that the functions are $\epsilon$-far if the number of points at which the functions $f$ and $g$ differ is atleast $\epsilon \cdot 2^n$. Mathematically, $f$ and $g$ are $\epsilon$-far if

$$|\{x \in \{0, 1\}^n : f(x) \neq g(x)\}| \geq \epsilon \cdot 2^n.$$

Further, a function $f$ is said to be $\epsilon$-far from a set $S$ of Boolean functions if $f$ is $\epsilon$-far from each of the Boolean function $g$ in $S$.

At this point, we know that the Walsh coefficient of an $n$-variate linear function of the form $f(x) = a \cdot x$ at a point $\omega$ can be given as

$$\hat{f}(\omega) = \begin{cases} 1 & \text{if } \omega = a \\ 0 & \text{if } \omega \neq a \end{cases}$$

In the classical setting, the linearity of a Boolean function can be performed using the Blum-Luby-Rubinfeld test or in short, the BLR test. It is known that any linear function $f(x)$ must satisfy $f(x \oplus y) = f(x) \oplus f(y)$. The BLR test is a probabilistic classical test that checks this condition, slightly modified to also incorporate affine functions. We describe this algorithm in Algorithm 3.1.

---

**Input**: A Boolean function $f$ on $n$ variables
**Output**: YES/NO

1 $b = f(0^n)$;
2 **for** $t$ *many times* **do**
3     Randomly choose distinct $x, y \in \{0, 1\}^n$;
4     Check the condition $f(x \oplus y) = b \oplus f(x) \oplus f(y)$;
5     **if** *the condition is not satisfied* **then**
       | report that $f$ is not affine (NO) and terminate;
    **end**
   **end**
6 Report that the function is affine (YES);

**Algorithm 3.1:** Classical algorithm for checking if a Boolean function is affine.

---

Let, for instance, an affine function $f(x) = a \cdot x \oplus b$ (for some secret $a$ and $b$) be given as input to the BLR test. Since the condition $f(x \oplus y) = f(0^n) \oplus f(x) \oplus f(y)$ is always satisfied, the test outputs that the function $f(x)$ is affine. On the other hand, if a non-affine function $g(x)$ is given as input to the test, the test could output NO if the randomly chosen $x, y$ are such that $f(x \oplus y) \neq f(x) \oplus f(y) \oplus f(0^n)$. But the test could also output YES in the event that none of the randomly chosen $x, y$ violate the equality condition. So, if the test reports NO, then the input function is certainly not linear. However, if the test reports YES, then the input function is linear with some probability. It can be shown that we can decide if a given function is $\epsilon$-far from the set of affine functions with probability 2/3 if we set $t = c\frac{1}{\epsilon}$ for a constant $c$ that comes out of the analysis of the BLR test. This analysis is quite involved and we ignore it for now for the benefit of the readers[2].

Let us now try to implement the classical BLR test using python. For the purpose of implementing the test, we use the 6-bit function $f(x) = x_1x_2 \oplus x_3x_4 \oplus x_5x_6$.

---

[2]The enthusiastic readers are directed towards [1] for the detailed proof.

```
1  #Importing the required classes and modules
2  from random import randint
3
4  #Defining a function that given an input x
5  #returns f(x)=x1x2+x3x4+x5x6
6  def func(x):
7      f = (int(x[0])*int(x[1]))+\
8      (int(x[2])*int(x[3]))+\
9      (int(x[4])*int(x[5]))
10     return f
11
12 #Defining a function that on input the Boolean
13 #function as func the size of the input to the
14 #Boolean function as n and the maximum number
15 #of iterations as t, returns if the given Boolean
16 #function is affine or not.
17 def BLR(func,n,t):
18     z = bin(0)[2:].zfill(n)
19     b = func(z)
20     for i in range(t):
21         x = randint(0,15)
22         y = randint(0,15)
23         while x==y:
24             y = randint(0,15)
25         xbin = bin(x)[2:].zfill(n)
26         ybin = bin(y)[2:].zfill(n)
27         xybin = bin(x^y)[2:].zfill(n)
28         if func(xybin) != (func(xbin)^func(ybin)^b):
29             return "Not Affine"
30     return "Affine"
31
32 print(BLR(func,6,10))
```

**Listing 3.3** Python code to perform BLR test on function $x_1x_2 \oplus x_3x_4 \oplus x_5x_6$

```
1  Output:
2  Not Affine
```

In Listing 3.3, we define two functions namely, func() that returns the value of $f(x)$ when given $x$ as input and BLR() that given a Boolean function func, the size of the input to func as n and a parameter t, returns as output if func is affine or not. If BLR() returns not affine then with certainty $f(x)$ is not affine. On the other hand if BLR() returns affine, then with high probability the output is correct. In the function BLR(), for t many times we perform the following: two random non-equal inputs $x$ and $y$ are obtained and their corresponding $f$ values are checked to see if the condition $f(x \oplus y) = f(x) \oplus f(y) \oplus f(0)$ holds. If the condition does not hold, then the function returns "Not Affine". If the condition holds for all the t iterations, then BLR() returns "Affine".

We can infer from the output that the function $f(x) = x_1x_2 \oplus x_3x_4 \oplus x_5x_6$ is not affine.

Now, that we have a probabilistic classical algorithm to test if a given function is affine or if it is $\epsilon$-far from the set of all affine functions that makes only $O(\frac{1}{\epsilon})$ queries to $f(x)$, the natural question that surfaces is if we can perform the same task with lesser number of queries on a quantum computer. What do you think? If at all we can perform better in a quantum setting, what tools can we use to provide an algorithm that can outperform the BLR test?

Well, let us first look at a quantum algorithm that performs a linearity test with the same query complexity as that of the BLR test. This quantum test uses the circuit of the Deutsch-Jozsa algorithm. It's algorithm is as given below.

---

**Input**: A Boolean function $f$ on $n$ variables
**Output**: YES/NO

1 Run the Deutsch-Jozsa algorithm except the final measurement;
2 Let $|\psi\rangle$ be the output state of the DJ algorithm;
3 Measure $|\psi\rangle$ in computational basis and store the output as $a_0$;
4 **for** $i = 1$ *to* $t$ **do**
5     Run the Deutsch-Jozsa algorithm except the final measurement;
6     Let $|\psi\rangle$ be the output state of the DJ algorithm;
7     Measure $|\psi\rangle$ in computational basis and store the output as $a_i$;
8     If $a_i \neq a_0$ Return NO (Not Affine);
   **end**
9 Return YES (Affine);

**Algorithm 3.2:** Quantum test for checking whether a Boolean function is affine.

---

Observe that similar to the classical case, the quantum test always outputs "affine" if the function is affine. However, if the given function is not affine then the algorithm may not always be correct. If the algorithm returns NO (not affine), then it is always correct, but if the algorithm returns YES (affine) then the given function is affine only with probability $1 - (1 - 2\epsilon)^{2t}$. This probability can be computed in the following manner. For any $\epsilon$-far function $f(x)$, we know that $f(x) \neq a \cdot x \oplus b$ for at least $\epsilon \cdot 2^n$ points for any $a \in \{0, 1\}^n$ and $b \in \{0, 1\}$. A direct consequence of this is that the normalized Walsh coefficient of the function $f(x)$ at any point $a$ satisfies $|\hat{f}(a)| \leq 1 - 2\epsilon$. Recall that the probability of observing $c$ as the output of the Deutsch-Jozsa algorithm is $|\hat{f}(c)|^2$. Thus, for any $i \neq 0$, the probability of obtaining $a_i = a_0$ is less than or equal to $(1 - 2\epsilon)^2$. Hence the probability of observing $a_i = a_0$ for all $i$ is less than or equal to $(1 - 2\epsilon)^{2t}$ in $t$ independent attempts, and this is the way the algorithm can mistakenly return YES for a non-affine function. If we choose $t = O(\frac{1}{\epsilon})$, then the error probability reduces to less than $\frac{1}{3}$. Observe that the query complexity of the quantum test, using only one repetition, i.e., $t = 1$, is same as that of the BLR test.

We now implement the quantum test for linearity in Qiskit. We perform the test on the 6-bit function $f(x) = x_1x_2 \oplus x_3x_4 \oplus x_5x_6$. The Qiskit implementation is done using the following code:

```
1  #Importing required classes and modules
2  from qiskit import *
3
4  #Defining a function that returns the oracle circuit
5  #of the Boolean function f(x) = x1x2+x3x4+x5x6.
6  def oracle():
7      orcl = QuantumCircuit(6)
8      orcl.cz(0,1)
9      orcl.cz(2,3)
10     orcl.cz(4,5)
11     return orcl.to_instruction()
12
13 #Defining a function that returns the output obtained
14 #on measuring the quantum circuit corresponding to
15 #implementing Deutsch-Jozsa algorithm on the zero
16 #state where the oracle is given by the  oracle()
17 #function
18 def DJ():
19     q = QuantumRegister(6)
20     c = ClassicalRegister(6)
21     qc = QuantumCircuit(q,c)
22
23     qc.h(range(6))
24     qc.append(oracle(),range(6))
25     qc.h(range(6))
26
27     for i in range(6):
28         qc.measure(i,5-i)
29
30     backend = Aer.get_backend('qasm_simulator')
31     qjob = execute(qc,backend,shots=1)
32     [res] = [val for val in qjob.result().get_counts()
       ]
33
34     return res
35
36 #Defining a function that takes as input the maximum
37 #number of iterations and returns if the given
38 #function is affine or not.
39 def q_lin_test(t):
40     a0 = DJ()
41     for i in range(t):
42         a = DJ()
43         if a!=a0:
44             return "Not Affine"
45     return "Affine"
46
47 test_res = q_lin_test(10)
48 print(test_res)
```

**Listing 3.4** Qiskit code for quantum linearity testing on function $x_1x_2 \oplus x_3x_4 \oplus x_5x_6$

```
1 Output:
2 Not Affine
```

The functions in the Qiskit code in Listing 3.4 are quite direct. `oracle()` returns the quantum oracle circuit for the function $f(x) = x_1x_2 \oplus x_3x_4 \oplus x_5x_6$. As conveyed earlier, the oracle for a function is generally given as a black box in practice. The function `DJ()` implements the Deutsch-Jozsa circuit on the $|0^n\rangle = |0^6\rangle$ state using the oracle given by `oracle()` and returns the state that is obtained on performing a single measurement. `q_lin_test()` on taking as input a parameter t, first obtains an output, say $a_0$, from `DJ()` and for t times obtain an output, say $a$ ,from `DJ()` and checks if $a_0 = a$. If $a_0 \neq a$ in any of the t iterations, then `q_lin_test()` outputs "Not Affine" else it returns "Affine".

The obtained output clearly indicates that the given function $f(x) = x_1x_2 \oplus x_3x_4 \oplus x_5x_6$ is not affine.

It is now time to look at a quantum algorithm that performs the linearity test but with a speedup. But before jumping into the algorithm, let us first do an analysis of the quantum test in Algorithm 3.2. Observe that the Algorithm 3.2 returns YES wrongly if in all the $t$ iterations we obtain $a_i = a_0$. So, if we could decrease the probability of obtaining the measurement outcome as $a_0$ or equivalently if we could increase the probability of obtaining the measurement outcome $a_i \neq a_0$, then we could reduce the error probability and thus the query complexity. We will see below that Grover's algorithm is just the right thing.

As discussed in the first section of this chapter, Grover's algorithm provides a way to increase the amplitude of the states of our interest. Let us now explore the possibility of using the Grover's algorithm to amplify the amplitudes of the basis states $|a_i\rangle \neq |a_0\rangle$. In Sect. 3.1, we introduced an operator called the Grover iterate given as $G = H^{\otimes n} U_{\bar{0}} H^{\otimes n} U_f$ where $U_{\bar{0}}$ is the oracle that acts as

$$U_{\bar{0}}|x\rangle = \begin{cases} |x\rangle & \text{if } |x\rangle = |0^{\otimes n}\rangle \\ -|x\rangle & \text{otherwise} \end{cases}.$$

and $U_f$ is an oracle that acts as

$$U_f|x\rangle = \begin{cases} -|x\rangle & \text{if } |x\rangle \text{ is a good state} \\ |x\rangle & \text{otherwise} \end{cases}.$$

For the current problem we use a modified Grover iterate which is given as $\hat{G} = AU_{\bar{0}}A^\dagger U_f$ where $A$ is an operator such that $A|0^n\rangle = |\psi\rangle = \sum_{x \in \{0,1\}^n} \hat{f}(x)|x\rangle$. And we further use $U_f$ that acts as

$$U_f|x\rangle = \begin{cases} -|x\rangle & \text{if } |x\rangle \neq |a_0\rangle \\ |x\rangle & \text{otherwise} \end{cases}.$$

This allows us to write the iterate $\hat{G}$ as $\hat{G} = AU_{\bar{0}}A^\dagger U_f = (2|\psi\rangle \langle\psi| - I)U_f$.

Now, the state $|\psi\rangle = \sum_{x \in \{0,1\}^n} \hat{f}(x) |x\rangle$ can be expressed as $\cos\theta |a_0\rangle + \sin\theta |\overline{a_0}\rangle$ where $\overline{a_0}$ contains all the computational basis states except the state $|a_0\rangle$. Consider applying the iterate $\hat{G}$ on the state $|\psi\rangle$. We can easily compute the output state to be $|\psi_1\rangle = \cos 3\theta |a_0\rangle + \sin 3\theta |\overline{a_0}\rangle$. Using induction, it is quite straight forward that on applying the iterate $\hat{G}$ $t$ times, we obtain the output state as $|\psi_1\rangle = \cos(2t+1)\theta |a_0\rangle + \sin(2t+1)\theta |\overline{a_0}\rangle$. The improved quantum algorithm for testing linearity is built on this behaviour. Consider the following quantum algorithm.

---

**Input**: A Boolean function $f$ on $n$ variables
**Output**: YES/NO

1 Let $|\psi\rangle$ be the output state of the Deutsch-Jozsa algorithm.;
2 Measure $|\psi\rangle$ in computational basis and store the output as $a_0$;
3 Construct the iterate $\hat{G} = (2 |\psi\rangle \langle\psi| - I)U_f$;
4 Apply $\hat{G}$ on $|\psi\rangle$ for $t$ times and measure the final state in computational basis. Let the output be $a_t$;
5 If $a_t \neq a_0$ Return NO (Not Affine) ;
6 Else return YES (Affine);

**Algorithm 3.3:** Better quantum test for checking if a Boolean function is affine.

---

In Algorithm 3.3, if the input function is an affine function, then the state $|\psi\rangle$ is of the form $|\psi\rangle = 1 \cdot |a_0\rangle + 0 \cdot |\overline{a_0}\rangle$. Hence, the iterate $\hat{G}$ does not have any effect on the state $|\psi\rangle$ and so the measurement output after $t$ iterations will be still be $|a_0\rangle$.

Alternatively, if the function in question is $\epsilon$-far from the set of affine functions, then we have the state $|\psi\rangle$ as $|\psi\rangle = \cos\theta |a_0\rangle + \sin\theta |\overline{a_0}\rangle$ where $\sin\theta > 0$. So, on applying $\hat{G}^t$ on $|\psi\rangle$, we obtain the state $|\psi_t\rangle = \cos(2t+1)\theta |a_0\rangle + \sin(2t+1)\theta |\overline{a_0}\rangle$ where $\sin^2(2t+1)\theta \geq \frac{2}{3}$. Thus, on measuring the state $|\psi_t\rangle$, we would obtain a measurement outcome $a_t \neq a_0$ with probability $\geq \frac{2}{3}$.

Algorithm 3.3 is complete once we determine the $t$ that would give us the optimal results. Note that $t$ does not have any effect if the given function is affine. So, we move to the other case, where we have $|\hat{f}(a_0)| \leq 1 - 2\epsilon$. Alternatively, in the state $|\psi\rangle = \cos\theta |a_0\rangle + \sin\theta |\overline{a_0}\rangle$, we have $\cos^2\theta \leq (1 - 2\epsilon)^2$. So $\sin\theta \geq \sqrt{1 - (1 - 2\epsilon)^2} = \sqrt{4\epsilon - 4\epsilon^2}$. Now, note that if a function $f(x)$ is $\epsilon$-far from a function $g(x)$, then $f(x)$ is also $1 - \epsilon$- far from the function $g(x) \oplus 1$. So when a function $f(x)$ is $\epsilon$-far from the set of all affine functions, it should be true that $1 - \epsilon \geq \epsilon$. This inequality holds only when $\epsilon \leq \frac{1}{2}$. So, we have $\sin\theta \geq \sqrt{4\epsilon - 4\epsilon^2} \geq \sqrt{2\epsilon}$. The last inequality comes from the fact that for $\epsilon < \frac{1}{2}$, $\sqrt{2(1 - \epsilon)} \geq 1$. We now need $t$ such that $\sin(2t+1)\theta \approx 1$ or $(2t+1)\theta \approx \frac{\pi}{2}$. Using the approximation $\sin\theta \approx \theta$ for small $\theta$ and the inequality $\sin\theta \geq \sqrt{2\epsilon}$ in obtaining $t$, we get $t = O(\frac{1}{\sqrt{\epsilon}})$. This is a quadratic speedup over the earlier quantum test!

Our next task is to implement the improved quantum test for linearity in Qiskit. We again run this test on the 6-bit Boolean function $f(x) = x_1 x_2 \oplus x_3 x_4 \oplus x_5 x_6$. The code for the implementation looks like the following:

```
1  #Importing the required classes and modules
2  from qiskit import *
3  from qiskit.circuit.library import *
4
5  #Defining a function that returns the oracle circuit
6  #of the Boolean function f(x) = x1x2+x3x4+x5x6.
7  def oracle():
8      orcl = QuantumCircuit(6)
9      orcl.cz(0,1)
10     orcl.cz(2,3)
11     orcl.cz(4,5)
12     return orcl
13
14 #Defining a function that returns the output obtained
15 #on measuring the quantum circuit corresponding to
16 #implementing Deutsch-Jozsa algorithm on the zero
17 #state where the oracle is given by the oracle()
18 #function
19 def DJ_w_meas(n):
20     q = QuantumRegister(n)
21     c = ClassicalRegister(n)
22     qc = QuantumCircuit(q,c)
23
24     qc.h(range(n))
25     qc.append(oracle(),range(n))
26     qc.h(range(n))
27
28     for i in range(n):
29         qc.measure(i,n-1-i)
30
31     backend = Aer.get_backend('qasm_simulator')
32     qjob = execute(qc,backend,shots=1)
33     [res] = [val for val in qjob.result().get_counts()
       ]
34
35     return res
36
37 #Defining a function that on input n returns the
38 #n-qubit quantum circuit that implements the
39 #Deutsch-Jozsa algorithm using the oracle given
40 #by the oracle() function.
41 def DJ_wo_meas(n):
42     q = QuantumRegister(n)
43     qc = QuantumCircuit(q)
44
45     qc.h(range(n))
46     qc.append(oracle(),range(n))
47     qc.h(range(n))
48
49     return qc
50
```

```
51  #Defining a function that on input a string x, returns
52  #an oracle for the Boolean function f(y)=0 if and
53  #only if y=x.
54  def cust_oracle(x):
55      orcl = QuantumCircuit(len(x))
56      if x[-1]=='0':
57          orcl.x(-1)
58      orcl.append(ZGate().control(len(x)-1, ctrl_state=x
        [::-1][1:]), range(len(x)))
59      if x[-1]=='0':
60          orcl.x(-1)
61      orcl.z(0)
62      orcl.x(0)
63      orcl.z(0)
64      orcl.x(0)
65      return orcl
66
67  #Defining a function that on input a string x returns
68  #the quantum circuit corresponding to the Grover's
69  #iterate that amplifies the amplitude of all the basis
70  #state except the state |x>.
71  def grover_iterate(x):
72      n = len(x)
73      qc = QuantumCircuit(n)
74      qc.append(cust_oracle(x), range(n))
75      qc.append(DJ_wo_meas(n).inverse(), range(n))
76      qc.x(-1)
77      qc.append(ZGate().control(n-1,ctrl_state='0'*(n-1)
        ),range(n))
78      qc.x(-1)
79      qc.append(DJ_wo_meas(n), range(n))
80
81      return qc
82
83  #We obtain the first output as reference and compare
84  #the next obtained output against a0.
85  a0 = DJ_w_meas(6)
86
87  #Creating a quantum circuit that applies the DJ
88  #circuit and amplifies all the basis states except
89  #the state |a0>.
90  qc = QuantumCircuit(6,6)
91  qc.append(DJ_wo_meas(6),range(6))
92
93  for i in range(2):
94      qc.append(grover_iterate(a0), range(6))
95
96  for j in range(6):
97      qc.measure(j,5-j)
98
99  #Executing the quantum circuit in simulator and
100 #obtaining the output.
101 backend = Aer.get_backend('qasm_simulator')
```

```
102 qjob  =  execute(qc,backend,shots=1)
103 [at]  =  [val for val in qjob.result().get_counts()]
104
105 if  at==a0:
106     print('Affine')
107 else:
108     print('Not Affine')
```

**Listing 3.5** Qiskit code for the improved quantum linearity test

```
1 Output:
2 Not Affine
```

The Qiskit code in Listing 3.5 can be thought of as an extension to Listing 3.4. Similar to the previous listing, we have defined an `oracle()` function that returns the quantum oracle circuit. We also define `DJ_w_meas()` that takes as input a parameter n, implements the Deutsch-Jozsa circuit on the state $|0\rangle^{\otimes n}$ and returns the state obtained on performing a single measurement. Along with these we also define a few more functions, namely `DJ_wo_meas()`, `cust_oracle()` and `grover_iterate()`. The function `DJ_wo_meas()` takes a parameter n as input and returns a circuit that implements the Deutsch-Jozsa circuit on the state $|0\rangle^{\otimes n}$. `cust_oracle` takes an input x and returns a quantum oracle circuit for the Boolean function $f(y) = 0 \iff y = x$. The `grover_iterate` function takes an input x and returns a quantum circuit that is the Grover iterate that amplifies the state $|x\rangle$.

Then, we obtain the output state, say $a_0$, of the function `DJ_w_meas()`. We then initialize a quantum circuit, say qc, and implement the Deutsch-Jozsa circuit on it by appending the circuit obtained as an output of the function `DJ_wo_meas`. Notice that at this point if we were to measure the circuit qc, we would obtain a state $|x\rangle$ with probability $|\hat{f}(x)|^2$. Next, we obtain the circuit for the Grover iterate using the function `grover_iterate()` with $a_0$ as input and append the same to qc some m many times. Subsequently, we measure the circuit qc once and check if the obtained output matches with $a_0$. If they match then we return "Affine" else we return "Not Affine". "Not Affine" here implies that the function is $\epsilon$ far from the set of affine functions where $\epsilon = O\left(\frac{1}{36}\right)$.

As the output of Listing 3.5 indicates, the given function $f(x) = x_1 x_2 \oplus x_3 x_4 \oplus x_5 x_6$ is not affine.

Linearity is one of the important properties of a Boolean function and not just from a cryptographic point of view. Linearity testing has direct consequences to the theory of NP-completeness, and problems in group theory and coding theory.

## 3.5  Resiliency

An n-bit Boolean function $f(x)$ is said to be m-resilient if the Walsh coefficient of $f(x)$ at all the n-bit strings of weight at most m are zero. The number of x such that $wt(x) \leq m$ can grow very large — exponential in n. This is easy to see since the number of $n$-bit strings with weight exactly $\frac{n}{2}$ is $\binom{n}{n/2} = \Theta(\frac{2^n}{\sqrt{n}})$. To ascertain if a Boolean function is $m$-resilient, a classical algorithm would have to compute $\hat{f}(x)$ for all $x$ with $wt(x) \leq m$ while verifying that all of them are zero and this is clearly going to be an exponential-time operation.

The immediate question that follows this analysis is the possibility of performing the same task better on a quantum computer. We know that the output state of the Deutsch-Jozsa algorithm is a superposition of the form

$$|\psi_f\rangle = \sum_{x \in \{0,1\}^n} \hat{f}(x) |x\rangle .$$

Can we use this state to determine if the given function is $m$-resilient? The following algorithm answers the question.

---

**Input**: A function $f$ on $n$ variables
**Input**: Order of resiliency $m$
**Input**: The number of iterations $r$
**Output**: YES/NO

1 **for** $r$ *many times* **do**
2      Let $|\psi\rangle$ denote the output state of the Deutsch-Jozsa circuit;
3      Measure $|\psi\rangle$ in the computational basis and store the output as $u$;
4      **if** $wt(u) \leq m$ **then**
        | Report that the function is not $m$-resilient (NO) and terminate;
     **end**
   **end**
5 Report that the function is (probably) $m$-resilient (YES);

**Algorithm 3.4:** Resiliency checking using Deutsch-Jozsa algorithm.

---

Now, we analyze the above algorithm. Define $S$ as the set $\{x \in \{0, 1\}^n : wt(x) \leq m\}$ and define $p$ to be a partial sum of the Walsh spectrum of $f(x)$ in the following manner.

$$p = \sum_{x \in S} \hat{f}^2(x)$$

Observe that the algorithm returns NO only when it manages to find some $u$ with weight at most $m$ and with non-zero $\hat{f}(u)$; thus, we can claim with certainty that the given function is not $m$-resilient.

Now consider the case when the algorithm returns YES. We want to analyze the probability of the algorithm making an error, i.e., the function was actually not $m$-resilient. The probability of obtaining a string $x \notin S$ is $1 - p$ for such a function. Then, the probability of obtaining a string $x \notin S$ in all of the $r$ iterations is $(1 - p)^r$.

It is tempting to set $r = c\frac{1}{p}$ for some suitable $c$ so that $(1 - p)^r \leq \frac{1}{3}$, and for this $r$ the algorithm answers correctly with probability at least $\frac{1}{3}$. Keep in mind that the query complexity in this case would be $\Theta(\frac{1}{p})$.

Unfortunately, this approach does not turn out to be efficient since $\hat{f}^2(a)$ can be as low as $\frac{4}{2^{2n}}$ when not zero; thus, it is possible to have $p$ as low as $\frac{4}{2^{2n}}$, in which case the query complexity of the algorithm is exponential similar to that of the classical algorithm. Therefore, this algorithm is no better that its classical counterpart in the worst case.

We saw above that it is not always easy to design a quantum algorithm that is better than a classical one. You may be wondering if there is a better way with a smaller query complexity compared to the classical test? Well, we can indeed perform better using the Grover's amplification algorithm along with the above quantum algorithm.

Recall the definition of $S$ from above and define $\overline{S}$ as the set of all the other $n$-bit strings. Define two (normalized) states

$$|X\rangle = \frac{\sum_{x:x\in S} \hat{f}(x)\,|x\rangle}{\sqrt{\sum_{x:x\in S} \hat{f}^2(x)}} \qquad |Y\rangle = \frac{\sum_{y:y\in\overline{S}} \hat{f}(y)\,|y\rangle}{\sqrt{\sum_{y:y\in\overline{S}} \hat{f}^2(y)}}$$

For our next algorithm, we start with the final state obtained from the Deutsch-Jozsa circuit and express it in terms of $|X\rangle$ and $|Y\rangle$.

$$|\psi\rangle = \sum_{x\in\{0,1\}^n} \hat{f}(x)\,|x\rangle = \sum_{x:x\in S} \hat{f}(x)\,|x\rangle + \sum_{y:y\in\overline{S}} \hat{f}(y)\,|y\rangle = a\,|X\rangle + b\,|Y\rangle$$

where $|a|^2 = \sum_{x:x\in S} \hat{f}^2(x) = \sin^2\theta$ and $|b|^2 = \sum_{y:y\in\overline{S}} \hat{f}^2(y) = \cos^2\theta$ for some $\theta$.

Notice that the states $\{|x\rangle \ : \ x \in S\}$ are precisely the states that we are interested in obtaining as measurement outcomes. If we could increase the probability of observing these states that will further increase the probability of our algorithm returning NO when the given function is actually not $m$-resilient. The trick to accomplish that lies in the Grover's algorithm.

We know that the Grover's iterate constitutes of two operations: a reflection about the bad states and a reflection about the initial state. The reflection about the bad states was accomplished by incorporating a negative phase on all the good states. Notice that this phase inversion can be performed by the oracle of a function which takes on value 1 if $|x\rangle$ is a good state and 0 otherwise. So, in our case, since any state whose weight is less than m is a good state, we use the oracle $U_g$ corresponding to the function $g(x)$ defined below.

$$g(x) = \begin{cases} 1 & \text{if } wt(x) \leq m \\ 0 & \text{else} \end{cases}$$

An important observation here is that $g(x)$ is symmetric. A symmetric function can be efficiently implemented by a classical circuit based on Boolean logic. More precisely, the circuit complexity of an $n$-bit symmetric function is $4.5n + O(n)$. Moreover, it is a well known result that a quantum circuit of comparable efficiency can be constructed to simulate any classical circuit. All of these put together, we can observe that it is possible to implement a quantum circuit that implements the oracle $U_g$ using polynomial in $n$ many gates. Now that we are assured that $U_g$ can be implemented efficiently, we move on with description of the algorithm.

Using $U_g$ to reflect about the bad states, we can now express the Grover iterate as $G = \left(2\,|\psi\rangle\,\langle\psi| - I\right)U_g$. On applying $G$ once on $|\psi\rangle$, we obtain the state $|\psi_1\rangle = \sin(3\theta)\,|X\rangle + \cos(3\theta)\,|Y\rangle$; observe the increase in the amplitudes (and probabilities) of the states corresponding to the strings with weight at most $m$. So, after $t$ applications of $G$, we would obtain a state of the form $|\psi_t\rangle = \sin((2t+1)\theta)\,|X\rangle + \cos((2t+1)\theta)\,|Y\rangle$. In order for us to maximize the benefit of Grover's amplification, we need to choose a $t$ such that $\sin((2t+1)\theta) \approx \sin(\frac{\pi}{2})$. A small calculation would reveal to us that this can happen if $t = O(\frac{1}{\theta})$. For large $n$, we can approximate $\theta = \sin\theta$ and hence, we get $t = O(\frac{1}{\sqrt{p}})$ since $p = sin^2\theta$. This is quite clearly a quadratic speedup over Algorithm 3.4. Notice that even in the worst case scenario when $p = O(\frac{1}{2^{2n}})$, using Grover's amplification we can obtain a good state with probability close to 1 in just $O(2^n)$ queries compared to the $O(2^{2n})$ many queries required in the classical approach in the worst case assuming the use of linear space.

Putting it all together, our improved quantum algorithm for testing if a given Boolean function is $m$-resilient is described below.

---

**Input**: An $n$-bit Boolean function $f$, available in the form of a unitary operator $U_f$
**Input**: Order of resiliency $m$
**Input**: Number of iterations $r$
**Input**: A series of positive integers $t_1, \ldots, t_r$ related to the number of Grover's iterations
**Output**: YES/NO

1  Compute $S = \{x \in \{0, 1\}^n \,|\, wt(x) \le m\}$;
2  **for** $i = 1$ *to* $r$ **do**
3      Apply Deutsch-Jozsa algorithm to obtain $|\psi\rangle = \sum_{x \in S} \hat{f}(x)\,|x\rangle + \sum_{y \notin S} \hat{f}(y)\,|y\rangle$ ;
4      By applying Grover's iteration, obtain $\left|\psi_{t_i}\right\rangle = [(2\,|\psi\rangle\,\langle\psi| - I)U_g]^{t_i}\,|\psi\rangle$;
5      Measure $|\Psi_{t_i}\rangle$ in the computational basis to obtain $n$-bit string $u$;
6      **if** $u \in S$ **then**
        | Report that the function is not $m$-resilient (NO) and terminate;
    **end**
  **end**
7  Report that the function is (probably) $m$-resilient (YES);

**Algorithm 3.5:** Resiliency checking using Grover's algorithm.

Algorithm 3.5 applies the Grover's iterate $t_i$ time at the $i^{th}$ iteration. The efficiency of the algorithm comes from carefully choosing the $t_i$ values which we now explain. We argued above that $t = O(\frac{1}{\sqrt{p}})$ many queries would be sufficient to amplify the probability of obtaining the states $x \in S$ upon measurement. However, we do not know the value of $p$ to start with. In fact, had we known the value of $p$ apriori then we could directly determine if the function is $m$-resilient or not. We face with an apparent ambiguity on the optimal choice of $t$.

We require a bit of analysis to resolve the crisis. Recall that our objective is to observe some state $x \in S$ if the given function is not $m$-resilient, or equivalently, the state after amplification should be of the form $\left| \psi_{t_i} \right\rangle = \sin \theta_i \left| X \right\rangle + \cos \theta_i \left| Y \right\rangle$ in which $\sin \theta_i$ is greater than or equal to some constant, say $c = \sin \theta_c$. This implies that we need some $t_i$ such that $\theta_c \leq (2t_i + 1)\theta \leq \pi - \theta_c$. Let us now divide the angular region $[0, \frac{\pi}{2}]$ into $r$ intervals as $\{(\alpha_{r+1}, \alpha_r], (\alpha_r, \alpha_{r-1}], \cdots, (\alpha_2, \alpha_1]\}$ where $0 = \alpha_{r+1} < \alpha_r < \cdots < \alpha_2 < \alpha_1 = \frac{\pi}{2}$. Now, if $\theta \in (\alpha_{i+1}, \alpha_i]$ then we need $t_i$ such that $\theta_c = (2t_i + 1)\alpha_{i+1} < (2t_i + 1)\theta < (2t_i + 1)\alpha_i = \pi - \theta_c$ — this has to hold for every $i$. Hence, we have the conditions on $\alpha_i$'s as

$$\theta_c = (2t_i + 1)\alpha_{i+1} \text{ and } (2t_i + 1)\alpha_i = \pi - \theta_c.$$

Similarly, we also have

$$\theta_c = (2t_{i-1} + 1)\alpha_i \text{ and } (2t_{i-1} + 1)\alpha_{i-1} = \pi - \theta_c.$$

From these two conditions, we get

$$\frac{2t_i + 1}{2t_i + 1} = \frac{\pi - \theta_c}{\theta_c}.$$

Using the initial condition as $t_1 = 0$ and solving the recurrence, we have

$$2t_i + 1 = \left( \frac{\pi - \theta_c}{\theta_c} \right)^{i-1}.$$

This determines the number of Grover's iterations $t_i$ required for the $i^{th}$ iteration. Using the values of $t_i's$, we choose the values of $\alpha_i's$ for $i = 2, \cdots, r$ such that the conditions $(2t_i + 1)\alpha_{i+1} < (2t_i + 1)\theta < (2t_i + 1)\alpha_i$ are not violated. Notice that the $t_i's$ are such that $t_i < t_{i+1}$ for all $i = 1, \cdots, r - 1$ and $t_r$ is such that $t_r = O(\frac{1}{\sqrt{p}})$ which is the number of Grover iterations in the worst case. Now, in the worst case, we have $\sin((2t_r + 1)\theta) \approx 1$ which implies $2t_r + 1 \approx \frac{\pi}{2\theta}$. Using the approximation that $\sin \theta \approx \theta$ for large $n$, we get $2t_r + 1 \approx \frac{\pi}{2 \sin \theta} = \frac{\pi}{2\sqrt{p}}$. As a consequence we have $\left( \frac{\pi - \theta_c}{\theta_c} \right)^{r-1} \approx \frac{\pi}{2\sqrt{p}}$. From this relation, we obtain $r$ as $r \approx \log_{\frac{\pi - \theta_c}{\theta_c}} \left( \frac{\pi}{2\sqrt{p}} \right)$ or $r = O\left( \log \left( \frac{1}{\sqrt{p}} \right) \right)$. This tells us that the Algorithm 3.5 makes at most $\log \left( \frac{1}{\sqrt{p}} \right)$ measurements. Now that we know the values of $t_i$'s and $r$, we will compute the total

number of queries made by the algorithm to the oracle of the given function. The
total number of queries can be expressed as

$$T = \sum_{i=1}^{r} t_i = \frac{1}{2} \sum_{i=1}^{r} \left( \left( \frac{\pi - \theta_c}{\theta_c} \right)^{i-1} - 1 \right).$$

Using a result from geometric progression and the fact that $\left( \frac{\pi - \theta_c}{\theta_c} \right)^{r-1} = 2t_r + 1 \approx$
$\frac{\pi}{2\theta}$,

$$T \approx \frac{1}{2} \left[ \frac{\frac{\pi}{2\theta} - 1}{(\frac{\pi - \theta_c}{\theta_c}) - 1} - \log^2 \left( \frac{\pi}{2\sqrt{p}} \right) \right].$$

Since $\frac{\pi - \theta_c}{\theta_c} > 1$, we finally have $T = O(\frac{1}{\theta}) = O(\frac{1}{\sqrt{p}})$.

So to summarise, if Algorithm 3.5 returns NO, then it is always correct and the
given function is not $m$-resilient. However, if the algorithm returns YES, then with
probability $p = 1 - \cos^{2r}((2t_r + 1)\theta)$ the given function is correctly identified to
be $m$-resilient. Using the values of $r = O(\log(\frac{1}{\sqrt{p}}))$ and $t_r = O(\frac{1}{\sqrt{p}})$, the success
probability turns out to be a constant.

Now, we show how to implement Algorithms 3.4 and 3.5 in Qiskit and try it on
the function $f(x) = x_1x_2 \oplus x_3x_4 \oplus x_5x_6$.

```
1  #Importing required classes and modules
2  from qiskit import *
3
4  #Defining a function that returns the oracle circuit
5  #of the Boolean function f(x) = x1x2+x3x4+x5x6.
6  def oracle():
7      orcl = QuantumCircuit(6)
8      orcl.cz(0,1)
9      orcl.cz(2,3)
10     orcl.cz(4,5)
11     return orcl.to_instruction()
12
13 #Defining a function that on input n returns the
14 #output obtained onmeasuring the n qubit quantum
15 #circuit corresponding to implementing Deutsch-Jozsa
16 #algorithm on the zero state where the oracle is
17 #given by the oracle() function
18 def DJ(n):
19     q = QuantumRegister(n)
20     c = ClassicalRegister(n)
21     qc = QuantumCircuit(q,c)
22
23     qc.h(range(n))
24     qc.append(oracle(),range(n))
25     qc.h(range(n))
26
```

```
27      for i in range(n):
28          qc.measure(i,n-1-i)
29
30      backend = Aer.get_backend('qasm_simulator')
31      qjob = execute(qc,backend,shots=1)
32      [res] = [val for val in qjob.result().get_counts()
        ]
33
34      return res
35
36  #Defining a function that performs the resiliency
37  #check as described in Algorithm 4.
38  def res_check_DJ(n,m,r):
39      for i in range(r):
40          u = DJ_with_meas(n)
41          wt_u = 0
42          for i in u:
43              wt_u += int(i)
44          if wt_u <= m:
45              return "Not "+str(m)+"-resilient"
46      return str(m)+"-resilient"
47  res_check_DJ(6,2,3)
```

**Listing 3.6**   Qiskit code to check resiliency using Deutsch-Jozsa algorithm

```
1  Output:
2  Not 2-resilient
```

The code in Listing 3.6 is a slight modification of the code in Listing 3.4. The functions oracle() and DJ() are exactly as defined in Listing 3.4. Along with those, we define the function res_check_DJ() that take three parameters n, m and r as input. In res_check_DJ(), for r many times we obtain output from DJ() with input n and check its weight against m. If the weight is less than m in some iteration then res_check_DJ() returns "Not m-resilient" else it returns "m-resilient". We then call res_check_DJ() with inputs n = 6, m = 2 and r = 3 to check if the function $f(x) = x_1 x_2 \oplus x_3 x_4 \oplus x_5 x_6$ is 2-resilient.

From the output of Listing 3.6, we can observe that the function $f(x) = x_1 x_2 \oplus x_3 x_4 \oplus x_5 x_6$ is not 2-resilient.

Next, we provide the Qiskit code to implement the improved quantum resiliency test on the same function that is $f(x) = x_1 x_2 \oplus x_3 x_4 \oplus x_5 x_6$.

```
1  #Importing the classes and modules
2  from qiskit import *
3  from qiskit.circuit.library import *
4  from qiskit.aqua.components.oracles import
       TruthTableOracle as tto
5
6  #Defining a function that returns the oracle circuit
7  #of the Boolean function f(x) = x1x2+x3x4+x5x6.
8  def oracle():
9      orcl = QuantumCircuit(6)
```

```
10      orcl.cz(0,1)
11      orcl.cz(2,3)
12      orcl.cz(4,5)
13      return orcl
14
15  #Defining a function that on input n returns the
16  #n-qubit quantum circuit that implements the
17  #Deutsch-Jozsa algorithm using the oracle given
18  #by the oracle() function.
19  def DJ_wo_meas(n):
20      q = QuantumRegister(n)
21      qc = QuantumCircuit(q)
22
23      qc.h(range(n))
24      qc.append(oracle(),range(n))
25      qc.h(range(n))
26
27      return qc
28
29  #Defining a function that on input n and m returns an
30  #quantum oracle circuit corresponding to the n-bit
31  #Boolean function f(x)=1 if and only if the Hamming
32  #weight of x is atmost m.
33  def weight_oracle(n,m):
34      g = ''
35      for i in range(2**n):
36          x = bin(i)[2:].zfill(n)
37          wt = 0
38          for j in range(n):
39              wt += int()
40          if wt <= m:
41              g+='1'
42          else:
43              g+='0'
44
45      return tto(g,optimization=True,mct_mode='noancilla
        ').circuit
46
47  #Defining a function that on input n and m returns the
48  #n qubit quantum circuit corresponding to the Grover's
49  #iterate that amplifies the amplitude of all the n bit
50  #bases states |x> where x is such that the Hamming
51  #weight of x is atmost m.
52  def grover_iterate(n,m):
53      qc = QuantumCircuit(n+1)
54      qc.x(-1)
55      qc.h(-1)
56      qc.append(weight_oracle(n,m), range(n+1))
57      qc.h(-1)
58      qc.append(DJ_wo_meas(n).inverse(), range(n))
59      qc.x(-1)
60      qc.append(ZGate().control(n,ctrl_state='0'*(n)),
        range(n))
```

```
61        qc.x(-1)
62        qc.append(DJ_wo_meas(n), range(n))
63
64        return qc
65
66 #Defining a function that on input n, m and a list t,
67 #returns if the n-bit Boolean function defined in
68 #oracle() is m-resilient or not.
69 def q_res_improv(n,m,t):
70     for i in range(len(t)):
71         qc = QuantumCircuit(n,n)
72         qc.append(DJ_wo_meas(n),range(n))
73         for j in range(t[i]):
74             qc.append(grover_iterate(n,m))
75         for k in range(n):
76             qc.measure(k,n-1-k)
77
78         backend = Aer.get_backend('qasm_simulator')
79         qjob = execute(qc,backend,shots=1)
80         [res] = [val for val in qjob.result().
       get_counts()]
81         wt_res = 0
82         for k in res:
83             wt_res += int(k)
84         if wt_res <= m:
85             return 'Not '+str(m)+'-resilient'
86     return str(m)+"-resilient"
87
88 #Setting m=4 to check if the function is 4-resilient.
89 n = 6
90 m = 4
91 t = [0,1,2,4]
92 print(q_res_improv(n,m,t))
```

**Listing 3.7** Qiskit code for the improved quantum resiliency test

```
1 Not 4-resilient
```

Similar to the previous listings, in Listing 3.7 we define a few functions first. We define `oracle()` and `DJ_wo_meas()` exactly as defined in Listing 3.5. We then define `weight_oracle()` that takes as input two parameters n and m and returns a quantum oracle circuit for the $n$-bit Boolean function $f(x) = 1 \iff wt(x) \le m$ where $wt()$ denotes the Hamming weight. We obtain the circuit using the `circuit()` method of the `TruthTableOracle()` class of Qiskit. Recall that given a binary input string $s$ of size $2^n$ as input, the `TruthTableOracle.circuit()` method returns a quantum oracle circuit for the $n$-bit Boolean function whose truth table string is $s$. We next define the `grover_iterate()` function. `grover_iterate()` takes as two input parameters as n and m and returns the Grover iterate circuit that amplifies the amplitudes of the states $|x\rangle$ where $x$ is such that $wt(x) \le m$. Notice that to reflect about the states $|x\rangle$ where $x$ is such that $wt(x) \le m$ in the Grover iterate, we use the `weight_oracle()` function. Lastly, we define the function `q_res_improv()` which on input n, m and t returns if the given $n$-bit Boolean function defined in `oracle()` is "m-resilient" or not using Algorithm 3.5. In the code above, since we have defined the oracle for the function $f(x) = x_1x_2 \oplus x_3x_4 \oplus x_5x_6$, on calling the function `q_res_improv()` with parameters n=6, m=4 and t=[0,1,2,4], it returns that $f(x)$ is not 4-resilient as seen in the output.

## Further Reading

The quantum search algorithm was proposed by Lov Grover in 1996 [8] soon after Peter Shor published his quantum algorithm to factor integers in 1994 [11]. Both of these algorithms introduced quantum computing to the world outside of research labs and academia as a useful and powerful alternative to conventional *aka.* classical style of computation. It is now understood that these two algorithms, as they were designed, have limited practical applicability but many new techniques and algorithms have been developed based on the principles that drive them. In this book, we focus on the *amplitude amplification* technique that is the workhorse that drives Grover's search algorithm. This technique was separately studied and made available as a general tool by Grover himself [9] and Brassard et al. [4, 5] independently.

The most well-known algorithm to identify nonlinear functions was designed by Blum et al. [3] and is known as the BLR algorithm. However, its detailed analysis came much later. Of particular importance is the technique proposed by Bellare et al. [1] based on the relationship of nonlinearity with Walsh coefficients. Recently the authors analysed the quantum version of the BLR algorithm and observed its limitations in estimating the nonlinearity of a Boolean function [2]. Similar quantum algorithms for testing linearity were earlier proposed by Hillery et al. [10] and Chakraborty et al. [6].

The algorithm that we described for computing resiliency of a Boolean function was designed by Chakraborty and Maitra [7] and is a typical example of combining amplitude amplification and the Deutsch-Jozsa algorithm, two very common subroutines in quantum algorithms for Boolean functions.

## References

1. Bellare, M., Coppersmith, D., Håstad, J., Kiwi, M., Sudan, M.: Linearity testing in characteristic two. IEEE Trans. Inf. Theory **42**(6), 1781–1795 (1996)
2. Bera, D., Maitra, S., Roy, D., Stănică, P.: Testing nonlinearity: limitation of the BLR testing and further results (extended abstract). In: Proceedings of the Eleventh International Workshop on Coding and Cryptography (2019)
3. Blum, M., Luby, M., Rubinfeld, R.: Self-testing/correcting with applications to numerical problems. J. Comput. Syst. Sci. **47**, 549–595 (1993). Preliminary version in STOC 1990

4. Brassard, G., Hoyer, P.: An exact quantum polynomial-time algorithm for Simon's problem. In: Proceedings of the Fifth Israeli Symposium on Theory of Computing and Systems, pp. 12–23. IEEE (1997)
5. Brassard, G., Hoyer, P., Mosca, M., Tapp, A.: Quantum amplitude amplification and estimation. Contemp. Math. **305**, 53–74 (2002)
6. Chakraborty, K., Maitra, S.: Improved quantum test for linearity of a Boolean function (2013). arXiv:1306.6195 [quant-ph]
7. Chakraborty, K., Maitra, S.: Application of Grover's algorithm to check non-resiliency of a Boolean function. Cryptogr. Commun. **8**(3), 401–413 (2016)
8. Grover, L.K.: A fast quantum mechanical algorithm for database search. In: Proceedings of the Twenty-eighth Annual ACM Symposium on Theory of Computing, pp. 212–219 (1996)
9. Grover, L.K.: Quantum computers can search rapidly by using almost any transformation. Phys. Rev. Lett. **80**(19), 4329 (1998)
10. Hillery, M., Andersson, E.: Quantum tests for the linearity and permutation in- variance of Boolean functions. Rev. A **84**(062329), 1–7 (2011)
11. Shor, P.W.: Algorithms for quantum computation: discrete logarithms and factoring. In: Proceedings 35th Annual Symposium on Foundations of Computer Science, pp. 124-134. IEEE (1994)

# Chapter 4
# Simon's Algorithm and Autocorrelation Spectrum

**Abstract** Simon's algorithm is another important evidence that more efficient evaluations of certain properties are possible in quantum domain over the classical paradigm. Given a vectorial Boolean function on $n$ variables that has certain periodicity, this algorithm is capable of obtaining the period in time complexity polynomial in $n$. In this chapter, we explain this algorithm in detail. Then we concentrate on the autocorrelation spectrum of a single output Boolean function and study how the quantum strategies fare in this domain. We present quantum algorithms to study the Walsh spectrum of higher order derivatives of a Boolean function. Examples and Qiskit codes are presented to explain the methods.

**Keywords** Autocorrelation spectrum · Boolean function · Simon's algorithm · Walsh spectrum

## 4.1 Simon's Algorithm

Suppose we are given a Boolean function $f(x) : \{0, 1\}^n \longrightarrow \{0, 1\}^k$ with a promise that for any two arbitrary inputs $x$ and $y$, $f(x) = f(y)$ if and only if $x = y \oplus s$ for some fixed $s \in \{0, 1\}^n$ and $k \geq \frac{n}{2}$. Our goal is to determine the shift $s$. This problem is known as the Simon's problem.

Using the method of compute and compare, a classical algorithm, in the worst case, would need to compute the function on atleast $\frac{2^n}{2} + 1$ different input strings to obtain two inputs that have the same functional output, and hence be able to determine $s$. But how hard is the problem for quantum computers? Similar to the problems discussed in the earlier chapters, is it possible to obtain a quantum algorithm that can solve the Simon's problem without making exponentially many queries to $f$? These questions are answered in the following discussion.

The Simon's algorithm efficiently uses the exclusive concepts of constructive and destructive interference available to quantum algorithms. Amazingly, it solves the problem making only $O(n)$ queries. Even though the algorithm applies to functions with an atypical promise, it reaffirms the claim that there exists a class of problems

T. SAPV et al., *Quantum Algorithms for Cryptographically Significant Boolean Functions*,
SpringerBriefs in Computer Science,
https://doi.org/10.1007/978-981-16-3061-3_4

**Fig. 4.1** Circuit for Simon's algorithm

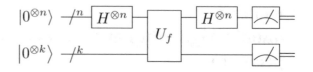

for which quantum algorithms can provide solutions exponentially faster than the best known classical algorithms.

The circuit for the Simon's algorithm is similar to that of the Deutsch-Jozsa algorithm except that the latter is used on Boolean functions with 1-bit output whereas the Simon's algorithm is used on Boolean functions that outputs multiple bits—we denote the number of bits by $k$. The quantum circuit corresponding to the Simon's algorithm is given in Fig. 4.1.

The evolution of the states after every layer in the circuit is calculated below.

$$|0^{\otimes n}\rangle |0^{\otimes k}\rangle \xrightarrow{H^{\otimes n}\otimes I} \frac{1}{\sqrt{2^n}} \sum_x |x\rangle |0^{\otimes k}\rangle$$

$$\xrightarrow{U_f} \frac{1}{\sqrt{2^n}} \sum_x |x\rangle |f(x)\rangle$$

$$\xrightarrow{H^{\otimes n}\otimes I} \frac{1}{2^n} \sum_x \sum_y (-1)^{x \cdot y} |y\rangle |f(x)\rangle$$

$$= \sum_y |y\rangle \otimes \left( \frac{1}{2^n} \sum_x (-1)^{x \cdot y} |f(x)\rangle \right)$$

The probability of observing a specific state $|y\rangle$ can be written as

$$Pr(|y\rangle) = \left\lVert \frac{1}{2^n} \sum_x (-1)^{x \cdot y} |f(x)\rangle \right\rVert^2.$$

Let us now analyze this probability for the different values of $s$.

**Case i** : Let $s = 0^{\otimes n}$. Notice that $f$ is one-to-one. The probability for this case is as calculated below.

$$Pr(|y\rangle) = \left\lVert \frac{1}{2^n} \sum_x (-1)^{x \cdot y} |f(x)\rangle \right\rVert^2$$

$$= \frac{1}{2^{2n}} \left\lVert \sum_x (-1)^{x \cdot y} |x\rangle \right\rVert^2 \text{ (since all } f(x) \text{ are distinct)}$$

$$= \frac{1}{2^n}$$

So, when the shift $s$ is $0^{\otimes n}$, we observe all the $2^n$ states in $\{|y\rangle \ : \ y \in \{0, 1\}^n\}$ with equal probability.

**Case ii** : Let $s \neq 0^{\otimes n}$. The probability of observing any $|y\rangle$ is now different. First define a set $A = \{f(x) \ : \ x \in \{0, 1\}^n\}$—this is the set of all the unique values of $f(x)$. Now, we can write

$$Pr(|y\rangle) = \left\lVert \frac{1}{2^n} \sum_{z \in A} \left((-1)^{x_1 \cdot y} + (-1)^{x_2 \cdot y}\right) |z\rangle \right\rVert^2$$

where $x_1 = x_2 \oplus s$ and $f(x_1) = f(x_2) = z$. Observe that $x_2 = x_1 \oplus s$ and so, $x_2 \cdot y = (x_1 \oplus s) \cdot y = (x_1 \cdot y) \oplus (s \cdot y)$. We can now simplify the expression further.

$$Pr(|y\rangle) = \left\lVert \frac{1}{2^n} \sum_{z \in A} \left((-1)^{x_1 \cdot y} + (-1)^{(x_1 \oplus s) \cdot y}\right) |z\rangle \right\rVert^2$$

$$= \left\lVert \frac{1}{2^n} \sum_{z \in A} (-1)^{x_1 \cdot y} \left(1 + (-1)^{s \cdot y}\right) |z\rangle \right\rVert^2$$

It is clear from the above expression that $Pr(|y\rangle) = 0$ for all $y$ such that $s \cdot y = 1$. This is an instance of destructive interference. On the other hand, for any $y$ satisfying $s \cdot y = 0$, we have $1 + (-1)^{y \cdot s} = 2$ which implies that $Pr(|y\rangle) = \frac{2}{2^n} = \frac{1}{2^{n-1}}$. This is an instance of constructive interference. We now arrive at the conclusion that on measuring the final state of the circuit given in Fig. 4.1, we always observe $|y\rangle$ such that $y \cdot s = 0$—in fact, the "y" we observe is chosen uniformly at random from all $y$'s that satisfy $y \cdot s = 0$.

The algorithm runs the circuit several times and takes $O(n)$ measurements to obtain $n$ distinct strings that we denote $y_1, y_2, \ldots, y_n$—all of those satisfy $y_i \cdot s = 0$. This gives us a system of $n$ linear equations with $n$ unknowns. If the $y_i \cdot s$ contain $n - 1$ linearly independent strings, then we can obtain the unknown string $s$ by solving this system of linear equations. It can be shown that the probability of obtaining such a set of linearly independent $y_i$'s is atleast $\frac{1}{4}$. That is, $O(n)$ measurements, and hence $O(n)$ queries, suffice to find the unknown shift $s$ with constant probability.

Now, let us implement the Simon's algorithm in Qiskit. Assume that we are given the following oracle of 3-bit Boolean function $f(x)$.

```
1  orcl = QuantumCircuit(6)
2  orcl.x(0)
3  orcl.ccx(0,2,5)
4  orcl.x([0,2])
5  orcl.ccx(0,2,3)
6  orcl.x(2)
7  orcl.ccx(0,1,3)
8  orcl.ccx(0,1,5)
9  oracle = orcl.to_instruction()
```

**Listing 4.1**  Qiskit code of the given oracle for solving Simon's problem

Moreover, we are also promised that for any two arbitrary inputs $x$ and $y$, $f(x) = f(y)$ if and only if $x = y \oplus s$ for some $s \in \{0, 1\}^3$. Our objective is to find $s$. We implement the Simon's algorithm using the following code:

```
1  #Importing classes and modules.
2  from qiskit import *
3
4  #Creating quantum register, classical register
5  #and quantum circuit.
6  q = QuantumRegister(6)
7  c = ClassicalRegister(3)
8  qc = QuantumCircuit(q,c)
9
10 #Implementing the quantum routine of the algorithm.
11 qc.h([q[0],q[1],q[2]])
12 qc.append(oracle, q)
13 qc.h([q[0],q[1],q[2]])
14 for i in range(3):
15     qc.measure(q[i],c[2-i])
16
17 #Executing the circuit in simulator.
18 backend = Aer.get_backend('qasm_simulator')
19 qjob = execute(qc,backend,shots=10)
20 counts = qjob.result().get_counts()
21 print(counts)
```
**Listing 4.2** Qiskit code for Simon's algorithm

```
1  Output:
2  {'101': 2, '001': 3, '100': 2, '000': 3}
```

From the output, we use the strings $y_1 = 101$, $y_2 = 001$ and $y_3 = 100$ to solve the system of linear equations given by $y_i \cdot s = 0$. This system of equations can be solved using methods like Gaussian elimination. In our case, on solving the system and verifying that $f(000) = f(010)$ corresponding to the two solutions we obtain, we see that the shift string $s$ is 010. Notice that if $f(000)$ was not equal to $f(010)$, then $s$ must have been 000.

## 4.2  Autocorrelation Transform

Similar to the Walsh-Hadamard transform that we studied in Chap. 2, the autocorrelation transform is another very important cryptographic tool used in the analysis of the Boolean functions, especially the $n$-bit to 1-bit functions. The autocorrelation transform of such a function represents the correlation among its values between all pairs of points at different distances. Consider a Boolean function $f : \{0, 1\}^n \longrightarrow \{0, 1\}$ and some point $a \in \{0, 1\}^n$. We define the autocorrelation coefficient of $f$ at $a$ in the following manner.

$$\Delta f(a) = \sum_{x \in \{0,1\}^n} (-1)^{f(x) \oplus f(x \oplus a)} \tag{4.1}$$

$\Delta f(a)$ can be perceived as the average correlation between the values of the function at $x$ and $x$ shifted by $a$, taken over all possible points $x$. The list of the autocorrelation coefficients at all the $2^n$ points,

$$\Delta f = [\Delta f(0), \Delta f(1), \cdots, \Delta f(2^n - 1)]$$

where $\Delta f(i)$ is the autocorrelation coefficient of $f(x)$ at the point whose decimal representation is $i$, is called the autocorrelation spectrum of the function $f(x)$. It should be observed that $\Delta f(0^n) = 2^n$—irrespective of $f$, and is therefore often ignored during analysis of a Boolean function.

In this section, we will show how to design algorithms for the autocorrelation spectrum. That will open the way for the other concepts like absolute indicator, avalanche criteria, etc. But the algorithm that we will discuss will require yet another property of Boolean functions—that of derivatives.

### 4.2.1 Higher-Order Derivatives

Higher-order derivatives of a Boolean function were explicitly introduced by Lai in the context of cryptanalysis.

---

**Definition 4.2.1: Derivative of a Boolean function**

The (first-order) derivative of an $n$-bit function $f : \{0, 1\}^n \longrightarrow \{0, 1\}$ in the direction of $a \in \{0, 1\}^n$ is defined as

$$\Delta f_a(x) = f(x \oplus a) \oplus f(x).$$

For a list of points $\mathcal{A} = (a_1, a_2, \ldots, a_k)$ (where $k \leq n$), the $k$-th derivative of $f$ at $(a_1, a_2, \ldots, a_k)$ is recursively defined as

$$\Delta f_{\mathcal{A}}^{(k)}(x) = \Delta f_{a_k}(\Delta f_{a_1,a_2,\ldots,a_{k-1}}^{(k-1)}(x)),$$

where $\Delta f_{a_1,a_2,\ldots,a_{k-1}}^{(k-1)}(x)$ is the $(k-1)$-th derivative of $f$ at points $(a_1, a_2, \ldots, a_{k-1})$. The 0-th derivative of $f$ is defined to be $f$ itself.

---

Higher-order derivatives form the basis of many cryptographic attacks, especially those that generalize the differential attack technique against block ciphers such as integral attack, AIDA, cube attack, zero-sum distinguisher etc. These attacks mostly revolve around the algebraic degree of a higher-order derivative. Let $deg(f)$ denote the algebraic degree of some function $f$. It is known that $deg(\Delta f^{(i+1)}) \leq deg(\Delta f^{(i)}) - 1$; this immediately means that $\Delta f^{(n)}$ is a constant function. Thus, if the degree of the $i$-th order derivative of a function at some $(a_1, a_2, \ldots a_i)$ to be a constant, then this fact is essentially a beacon for mounting an attack, especially, if

$i \ll n$. These sort of attacks is one motivation to study the algebraic degree and the other properties of higher-order derivatives. First, we show how to efficiently sample from the Walsh-Hadamard spectrum of the $i$-th order derivative, for any given $i$. This allows us to estimate if any higher-order derivative of $f$ is biased towards any linear function.

Despite the complicated expression for computing $\Delta f^{(k)}$, it has an equivalent expression that comes handy. For any multiset $S$ of points from $\{0, 1\}^n$ (including $S = \emptyset$), define the notation $f(x \oplus S) = f(x \oplus \bigoplus_{a \in S} a)$; we define $f(x \oplus S) = f(x)$ when $S$ is empty. With the help of a little algebra, the $i$-th derivative of $f$ at $\mathcal{A} = (a_1, a_2, \ldots a_i)$ can be shown to be

$$\Delta f_{\mathcal{A}}^{(i)}(x) = \bigoplus_{S \subseteq A} f(x \oplus S)$$

where $S \subseteq A$ indicates all possible sub-lists of $\mathcal{A}$ (including duplicates, if any, in $\mathcal{A}$) [5]. For example, the second-order derivative at a pair of points $(a, b)$ can be written as

$$\Delta f_{(a,b)}^{(2)} = f(x) \oplus f(x \oplus a) \oplus f(x \oplus b) \oplus f(x \oplus a \oplus b).$$

For the sake of brevity, we will drop the superscript $(i)$ if it is clear from the list $\mathcal{A}$.

Now, we describe a quantum circuit that generates the Walsh-Hadamard spectrum of the $k$-derivative of an $n$-bit function $f$ at some set of points $\mathcal{A} = (a_1, a_2, \ldots a_k)$. We refer to the circuit as $HoDJ_n^k$ ("Higher-order Deutsch-Jozsa" due to its similarity to the Deutsch-Jozsa circuit).

We use $|+\rangle$ and $|-\rangle$ to denote the states $\frac{1}{\sqrt{2}}(|0\rangle + |1\rangle)$ and $\frac{1}{\sqrt{2}}(|0\rangle - |1\rangle)$, respectively. Observe that $U_f |x\rangle |+\rangle = |x\rangle |+\rangle$ and $U_f |x\rangle |-\rangle = (-1)^{f(x)} |x\rangle |-\rangle$.

The circuit for $HoDJ_n^k$ acts on $k + 2$ registers, $R_1, \ldots R_k, R_{k+1}, R_{k+2}$ that are initialized as:

- $R_1$ has one qubit that is initialized to $|1\rangle$,
- $R_2$ consists of $n$-qubits that are initialized to $|0^n\rangle$,
- and each of $R_3 \ldots R_{k+2}$ consists of $n$-qubits of which $R_{2+t}$ is initialized to the state $|a_t\rangle$ of $\mathcal{A}$.

The circuit itself is a generalization of the quantum circuit for the Deutsch-Jozsa problem [3] and uses the ability of the latter circuit to generate a distribution of Walsh-Hadamard coefficients that was explained earlier.

Figure 4.2 shows the quantum circuit for $HoDJ_n^1$; for this problem, $\mathcal{A}$ is a singleton set, say $\{a\}$. The evolution of the quantum state as the operators are applied is as follows:

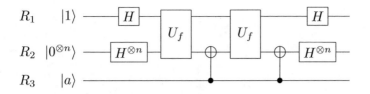

**Fig. 4.2** Circuit for 1st-order Walsh-Hadamard derivative sampling

$$\text{Initial State}: \ |1\rangle \, |0^n\rangle \, |a\rangle$$

$$\xrightarrow{H \otimes H^n} \frac{1}{\sqrt{2^n}} \sum_x |-\rangle \, |x\rangle \, |a\rangle$$

$$\xrightarrow{U_f} \frac{1}{\sqrt{2^n}} \sum_x (-1)^{f(x)} |-\rangle \, |x\rangle \, |a\rangle$$

$$\xrightarrow{CNOT_2^3} \frac{1}{\sqrt{2^n}} \sum_x (-1)^{f(x)} |-\rangle \, |x \oplus a\rangle \, |a\rangle$$

$$\xrightarrow{U_f} \frac{1}{\sqrt{2^n}} \sum_x (-1)^{f(x) \oplus f(x \oplus a)} |-\rangle \, |x \oplus a\rangle \, |a\rangle$$

$$\xrightarrow{CNOT_2^3} \frac{1}{\sqrt{2^n}} |-\rangle \sum_x (-1)^{f(x) \oplus f(x \oplus a)} |x\rangle \, |a\rangle$$

$$\xrightarrow{H \otimes H^n} |1\rangle \sum_y \left[ \frac{1}{2^n} \sum_x (-1)^{(x \cdot y)} (-1)^{f(x) \oplus f(x \oplus a)} \right] |y\rangle \, |a\rangle$$

$$= |1\rangle \sum_y \widehat{\Delta f_a}(y) \, |y\rangle \, |a\rangle$$

Therefore, at the end of the circuit $R_2$ can be found to be in a state $|y\rangle$ with probability $\widehat{\Delta f_a}(y)^2$ thus accomplishing the objective of sampling according to the Walsh-Hadamard distribution of the 1st-order derivative of $f$.

We now present the Qiskit code to obtain the Walsh distribution of the 1st order derivative of a given Boolean function.

```
#Importing the required classes and modules
from qiskit import *
from qiskit.circuit.library import *

#Defining the oracle for the function f(x)=x1+x1x2+x1x2x3
    +x1x2x3x4
def oracle():
    circ = QuantumCircuit(4)
    circ.z(0)
    circ.cz(0,1)
    circ.append(ZGate().control(2),range(3))
    circ.append(ZGate().control(3),range(4))
```

```
12      return circ
13
14  #Defining the size of the input to the Boolean
15  #function f(x) and the sampling point a
16  n = 4
17  a = '0100'
18
19  #Constructing a quantum circuit and implementing gates as
20  #described in Algorithm
21  qc = QuantumCircuit(2*n,n)
22  for i in range(len(a)):
23      if a[i]=='1':
24          qc.x(n+i)
25  qc.h(range(n))
26  qc.append(oracle(),range(n))
27  qc.cx(range(n,2*n),range(n))
28  qc.append(oracle(),range(n))
29  qc.cx(range(n,2*n),range(n))
30  qc.h(range(n))
31
32  #Measuring the first n qubits
33  for i in range(n):
34      qc.measure(i,n-i-1)
35
36  #Executing the quantum circuit in a simulator
37  backend = Aer.get_backend('qasm_simulator')
38  shots = 8000
39  job = execute(qc,backend,shots=shots)
40  counts = job.result().get_counts()
41
42  #Constructing the list of the estimates of the
43  #First-Order Walsh derivatives at the point a
44  wd = []
45  for i in range(2**n):
46      ind = bin(i)[2:].zfill(n)
47      if ind in counts:
48          wd.append(counts[ind]/shots)
49      else:
50          wd.append(0)
51  print("The estimate of the squared Walsh spectrum of the
        First-Order Derivative spectrum at the point " + a + "
        is :")
52  print(wd)
```

**Listing 4.3** Qiskit code to obtain Walsh distribution of the 1st order derivative of f at the point 0100

```
1  Output:
2  The estimate of the squared Walsh spectrum of the
      First-Order Derivative spectrum at the point 0100
      is :
3  [0.0625, 0.0625, 0.0625, 0.0625, 0.0, 0.0, 0.0, 0.0,
      0.5625, 0.0625, 0.0625, 0.0625, 0.0, 0.0, 0.0, 0.0]
```

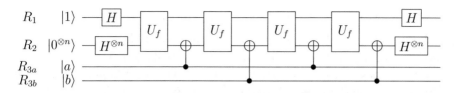

**Fig. 4.3** Circuit for Walsh-Hadamard sampling of 2nd-order derivative

The code in Listing 4.3 is quite straightforward. We first define the oracle circuit for the function $f(x) = x_1 \oplus x_1 x_2 \oplus x_1 x_2 x_3 \oplus x_1 x_2 x_3 x_4$ in the function `oracle()`. We then set the size of input of $f(x)$ as 4 and the point $a$ as 0100. Following this, we merely create and implement the circuit as in Fig. 4.2. Once the circuit is implemented, we obtain and return the probability estimate of each of the points. The array of the probability estimates of the points clearly correspond to the square of the Walsh spectrum of the 1st order derivative of $f(x)$ at the point 0100.

Next, an illustration of $HoDJ_n^2$ corresponding to the 2nd-order derivative is presented in Fig. 4.3 in which we use $\mathcal{A} = (a, b)$. We show the state of this circuit after each layer of operators below.

$$\text{Initial State}: \ |1\rangle \left|0^n\right\rangle |a\rangle |b\rangle$$

$$\xrightarrow{H \otimes H^n} \ \frac{1}{\sqrt{2^n}} \sum_{x \in \{0,1\}^n} |-\rangle |x\rangle |a, b\rangle$$

$$\xrightarrow{U_f} \ \frac{1}{\sqrt{2^n}} \sum_x (-1)^{f(x)} |-\rangle |x, a, b\rangle$$

$$\xrightarrow{CNOT_2^3} \ \frac{1}{\sqrt{2^n}} \sum_x (-1)^{f(x)} |-\rangle |x \oplus a\rangle |a, b\rangle$$

$$\xrightarrow{U_f} \ \frac{1}{\sqrt{2^n}} \sum_x (-1)^{f(x) \oplus f(x \oplus a)} |-\rangle |x \oplus a\rangle |a, b\rangle$$

$$\xrightarrow[U_f]{CNOT_2^4,} \ \frac{1}{\sqrt{2^n}} \sum_x (-1)^{f(x) \oplus f(x \oplus a) \oplus f(x \oplus a \oplus b)} |-\rangle |x \oplus a \oplus b\rangle |a, b\rangle$$

$$\xrightarrow[U_f]{CNOT_2^3} \ \frac{1}{\sqrt{2^n}} \sum_x (-1)^{f(x) \oplus f(x \oplus a) \oplus f(x \oplus b) \oplus f(x \oplus a \oplus b)} |-\rangle |x \oplus b\rangle |a, b\rangle$$

$$\xrightarrow{CNOT_2^4} \ \frac{1}{\sqrt{2^n}} \sum_x (-1)^{\oplus_{S \subseteq \{a,b\}} f(x \oplus S)} |-\rangle |x, a, b\rangle$$

$$\xrightarrow{H \otimes H^n} \ |1\rangle \sum_y \left[ \frac{1}{2^n} \sum_x (-1)^{x \cdot y} (-1)^{\oplus_{S \subseteq \{a,b\}} f(x \oplus S)} \right] |y\rangle |a, b\rangle$$

Measuring $R_2$ at the end will collapse it into $|y\rangle$ for some $y \in \{0, 1\}^n$ with probabil-
ity $\Pr[y] = \left[ \frac{1}{2^n} \sum_x (-1)^{x \cdot y} \Delta f_{(a,b)}(x) \right]^2 = \widehat{\Delta f_{(a,b)}}(y)^2$ that is the square of the Walsh
coefficient of $\Delta f_{(a,b)}$ (2nd-order derivative function) at the point $y$.

Next, we present the code the creates a quantum circuit to obtain the Walsh
distribution of the 2nd order derivative of the function $f(x) = x_1 \oplus x_1 x_2 \oplus x_1 x_2 x_3 \oplus x_1 x_2 x_3 x_4$ at the points $a = 0100$ and $b = 0011$.

```python
#Importing the required classes and modules
from qiskit import *
from qiskit.circuit.library import *

#Defining the oracle for the function f(x)=x1+x1x2+
    x1x2x3+x1x2x3x4
def oracle():
    circ = QuantumCircuit(4)
    circ.z(0)
    circ.cz(0,1)
    circ.append(ZGate().control(2),range(3))
    circ.append(ZGate().control(3),range(4))
    return circ

#Defining the size of the input to the Boolean
#function f(x) and the sampling point a
n = 4
a = '0100'
b = '0011'

#Constructing a quantum circuit and implementing gates
#as described in Algorithm
qc = QuantumCircuit(3*n,n)
for i in range(len(a)):
        if a[i]=='1':
            qc.x(n+i)
        if b[i]=='1':
            qc.x((2*n)+i)
qc.h(range(n))
qc.append(oracle(),range(n))
qc.cx(range(n,2*n),range(n))
qc.append(oracle(),range(n))
qc.cx(range(2*n,3*n),range(n))
qc.append(oracle(),range(n))
qc.cx(range(n,2*n),range(n))
qc.append(oracle(),range(n))
qc.cx(range(2*n,3*n),range(n))
qc.h(range(n))

#Measuring the first n qubits
for i in range(n):
        qc.measure(i,n-i-1)

```

```
43  #Executing the quantum circuit in a simulator
44  backend = Aer.get_backend('qasm_simulator')
45  shots = 8000
46  job = execute(qc,backend,shots=shots)
47  counts = job.result().get_counts()
48
49  #Constructing the list of the estimates of the
50  #Second-Order Walsh derivatives at the point a
51  wd = []
52  for i in range(2**n):
53      ind = bin(i)[2:].zfill(n)
54      if ind in counts:
55          wd.append(counts[ind]/shots)
56      else:
57          wd.append(0)
58  print("The estimate of the squared Walsh spectrum of
        the Second-Order Derivative at the point " + a + "
        and " + b + " is :")
59  print(wd)
```

**Listing 4.4**  Qiskit code to obtain Walsh distribution of the 2nd order derivative of f at the points 0100 and 0011

```
1  Output:
2  The estimate of the Walsh coefficients of the Second-
       Order Derivative spectrum at the point 0100 and
       0011 is :
3  [0.251, 0, 0, 0.248625, 0, 0, 0, 0, 0.25, 0, 0,
       0.250375, 0, 0, 0, 0]
```

Let us now understand the code in Listing 4.4. Similar to Listing 4.3, the code is simple. We first define the oracle circuit of the function $f(x) = x_1 \oplus x_1 x_2 \oplus x_1 x_2 x_3 \oplus x_1 x_2 x_3 x_4$ in oracle(). We then construct the circuit as in Fig. 4.3 and run it the qasm_simulator. Finally, we obtain an array containing the proportion of each of the strings obtained in the output and report it as the estimate of the square of the Walsh spectrum of $\Delta f_{(a,b)}(x)$ where $a = 0100$ and $b = 0011$.

The circuit can be generalized to higher values of $k$ in a straight forward manner. The following theorem formalizes this result where we ignore the first register since that contains an ancillary qubit which is reset to its initial state at the end of the computation. For counting the number of gates, please note that each of the CNOT gates shown in Fig. 4.3 actually consists of $n$ 2-qubit CNOT gates applied in parallel.

**Theorem 4.1**  *For any $\mathcal{A} = (a_1, a_2, \ldots a_k)$ such that $a_i \in \{0, 1\}^n$ $\forall i$, the $HoDJ_n^k$ circuit uses $n + 1$ initialized ancilla qubits, employs $k$ registers corresponding to the points in $\mathcal{A}$, makes $2^k$ calls to $U_f$, $\Theta(n2^k)$ calls to H and CNOT gates, has a depth of $2(2^k + 1)$ and operates as follows*

$$|0^n\rangle |a_1\rangle \ldots |a_k\rangle \xrightarrow{HoDJ_n^k} \sum_y \widehat{\Delta f_{\mathcal{A}}}(y) |y\rangle |a_1\rangle \ldots |a_k\rangle$$

**Proof** The circuit is a generalization of those illustrated in Figs. 4.2 and 4.3. At the core is a sub-circuit that we denote by $C'$ and which acts as

$$|x\rangle |a_1\rangle \ldots |a_k\rangle |b\rangle \xrightarrow{C'} |x\rangle |a_1\rangle \ldots |a_k\rangle |b \oplus \Delta f_{\mathcal{A}}\rangle (x)$$

$$= |x\rangle |a_1\rangle \ldots |a_k\rangle \left| b \oplus \bigoplus_{S \subseteq \mathcal{A}} f(x \oplus S)\right\rangle .$$

Construction of $C'$ uses a *binary reflected Gray code* (BRGC, or "Gray code" in short) for the set of integers $\{0, 1, \ldots, 2^k - 1\}$. Such a BRGC will be a sequence of $k$-bit strings (codes) $(g_1, g_2, \ldots, g_{2^k})$ such that each $g_i$ is unique and every adjacent code differ at exactly one position. Integer 0 is encoded by the code $0^n$ and without loss of generality, let $g_{2^k} = 0^n$. Due to the cyclic property of BRGC, $g_1$ must be some $k$-bit string with Hamming weight 1.

$C'$ operates in $2^k$ stages. We will use $|\mathcal{A}\rangle$ as a shorthand for $|a_1\rangle \ldots |a_k\rangle$. The initial state of the qubits, before stage 1, is $|x\rangle |\mathcal{A}\rangle |b\rangle$. Observe that $\bigoplus_{S \subseteq \mathcal{A}} f(x \oplus S) = \bigoplus_{i=1}^{2^k} f(x \oplus (g_i \cdot \mathcal{A}))$ in which we used the notation $g_j \cdot \mathcal{A} = (g_j)_1 a_1 \oplus (g_j)_2 a_2 \oplus \ldots \oplus (g_j)_k a_k$ to denote a linear combination of some of the $a_i$'s.

The $j$-th stage of $C'$ creates the state $\left| x \oplus (g_j \cdot \mathcal{A})\right\rangle |\mathcal{A}\rangle \left| b \oplus \bigoplus_{i=1}^{j} f(g_i \cdot \mathcal{A})\right\rangle$ by making the following transformations.

$$\left| x \oplus (g_{j-1} \cdot \mathcal{A})\right\rangle |\mathcal{A}\rangle \left| b \oplus \bigoplus_{i=1}^{j-1} f(g_i \cdot \mathcal{A})\right\rangle$$

$$\xrightarrow{CNOT} \left| x \oplus (g_j \cdot \mathcal{A})\right\rangle |\mathcal{A}\rangle \left| b \oplus \bigoplus_{i=1}^{j-1} f(g_i \cdot \mathcal{A})\right\rangle$$

$$\xrightarrow{U_f} \left| x \oplus (g_j \cdot \mathcal{A})\right\rangle |\mathcal{A}\rangle \left| b \oplus \bigoplus_{i=1}^{j-1} f(g_i \cdot \mathcal{A}) \oplus f(g_j \cdot \mathcal{A})\right\rangle$$

The $CNOT$ operation above is justified since $g_{j-1} \cdot \mathcal{A}$ and $g_j \cdot \mathcal{A}$ are both linear combinations of some of the $a_i$'s differing by exactly one $a_t$. The $CNOT$ uses the corresponding register $|a_t\rangle$ as the control register and the first register qubit as the target register. This also holds true for stage 1 since $g_1$ has Hamming weight 1. Lastly, observe that the final state after the $2^k$-th stage matches the one specified above: $|x\rangle |\mathcal{A}\rangle \left| b \oplus \bigoplus_{S \subseteq \mathcal{A}} f(x \oplus S)\right\rangle$.

It is not hard to calculate that $C'$ also makes the following transformation if $|b\rangle$ is replaced by $|-\rangle$.

$$|x\rangle |a_1 \ldots a_k\rangle |-\rangle \xrightarrow{C'} (-1)^{\oplus_{S \subseteq \mathcal{A}} f(x \oplus S)} |x\rangle |a_1 \ldots a_k\rangle |-\rangle$$

$$= (-1)^{\Delta f_{\mathcal{A}}(x)} |x\rangle |a_1 \ldots a_k\rangle |-\rangle$$

The circuit for $HoDJ_n^k$ is constructed as

$$|-\rangle |0^n\rangle |a_1 \ldots a_k\rangle$$

$$\xrightarrow{H^n} \frac{1}{\sqrt{2^n}} \sum_x |-\rangle |x\rangle |a_1 \ldots a_k\rangle$$

$$\xrightarrow{C'} \frac{1}{\sqrt{2^n}} \sum_x |-\rangle (-1)^{\Delta f_{\mathcal{A}}(x)} |x\rangle |a_1 \ldots a_k\rangle = |-\rangle \frac{1}{\sqrt{2^n}} \sum_x (-1)^{\Delta f_{\mathcal{A}}(x)} |x\rangle |a_1 \ldots a_k\rangle$$

$$\xrightarrow{H^n} |-\rangle \sum_y \widehat{\Delta f_{\mathcal{A}}}(y) |y\rangle |a_1 \ldots a_k\rangle$$

For computing the resource usage of $HoDJ_n^k$, observe that $C'$ is implemented above using a depth $2 \cdot 2^k$ circuit and each of its stages employ one $U_f$ gate and $n$ CNOT gates (that act in parallel on all the $n$ qubits of the first register and is shown as a single CNOT operation above). This completes the proof of the theorem.

A quick observation is that the circuit for $HoDJ_n^0$ is exactly same as that of the Deutsch-Jozsa circuit for $n$-bit functions.

### 4.2.2 Algorithm for Autocorrelation Sampling

Moving on, now we present an algorithm to sample according to a distribution that is proportional to the autocorrelation coefficients of a function; specifically, we would like to output $|a\rangle$ with probability proportional to $\Delta f(a)^2$.

An algorithm for this task is described in Algorithm 4.1 and the corresponding circuit, except the amplitude amplification part, is illustrated in Fig. 4.4. Suppose we run the circuit, perform a measurement in the standard basis and observe some $n$-bit string in $R_3$ that we denote $a$. We will show that the probability of observing $a$ is actually $\Delta f(a)^2/\sigma_f$ with probability at least $1 - \delta$. Here we used $\sigma_f$ to denote $\sum_a \Delta f(a)^2$. We will further show that the algorithm makes $O(\frac{2^{n/2}}{\sqrt{\sigma_f}} \log \frac{2}{\delta})$ queries to $U_f$ and uses $O(n \frac{2^{n/2}}{\sqrt{\sigma_f}} \log \frac{2}{\delta})$ gates altogether.

We will use the technique presented in Sect. 4.2.1 for doing so. We start with a simple identity.

$$\Delta f(a) = \widehat{\Delta f_a^{(1)}}(0^n) \tag{4.2}$$

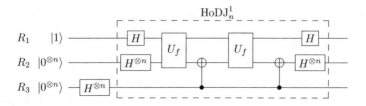

**Fig. 4.4** Circuit for autocorrelation sampling

To prove the identity we first expand the LHS as $\frac{1}{2^n}\sum_x(-1)^{f(x)}(-1)^{f(x\oplus a)} = \frac{1}{2^n}\sum_x(-1)^{\widehat{\Delta f_a^{(1)}(x)}}$. Then, we expand the RHS as $\widehat{\Delta f_a^{(1)}}(0^n) = \frac{1}{2^n}\sum_x(-1)^{\Delta f_a^{(1)}(x)}$ which matches the expansion of the LHS.

---

1: Start with three registers initialized as $|1\rangle$, $|0^n\rangle$, and $|0^n\rangle$.

2: Apply $H^n$ to $R_3$ to generate the state $\frac{1}{\sqrt{2^n}}\sum_{b\in\mathbb{F}_2^n}|1\rangle\,|0^n\rangle\,|b\rangle$.

3: Apply $HoDJ_n^1$ on the registers $R_1$, $R_2$ and $R_3$ to generate the state
$$|\Phi\rangle = \frac{1}{\sqrt{2^n}}|1\rangle\sum_{b\in\mathbb{F}_2^n}\sum_{y\in\mathbb{F}_2^n}\widehat{\Delta f_b^{(1)}}(y)\,|y\rangle\,|b\rangle.$$

4: Apply amplitude amplification on $|\Phi\rangle$ to amplify the probability of observing $R_2$ in the state $|0\rangle$ to $1-\delta$ for any given constant $\delta$.

5: Measure $R_3$ in the standard basis and return the observed outcome.

**Algorithm 4.1:** Algorithm for autocorrelation sampling

---

Next, we analyse the output distribution of the circuit. We will begin by calculating the final state that we denote $|\Phi\rangle$.

$$|\Phi\rangle = \frac{1}{\sqrt{2^n}}|1\rangle\sum_{b\in\mathbb{F}_2^n}\sum_{y\in\mathbb{F}_2^n}\widehat{\Delta f_b^{(1)}}(y)\,|y\rangle\,|b\rangle$$

$$= |1\rangle\otimes|0^n\rangle\otimes\left(\frac{1}{\sqrt{2^n}}\sum_b\widehat{\Delta f_b}(0^n)\,|b\rangle\right) + \sum_{y\neq 0^n}|1\rangle\,|y\rangle\otimes\left(\frac{1}{\sqrt{2^n}}\sum_b\widehat{\Delta f_b}(y)\,|b\rangle\right)$$

$$= |1\rangle\otimes|0^n\rangle\otimes\left(\frac{1}{\sqrt{2^n}}\sum_b\Delta f(b)\,|b\rangle\right) + \sum_{y\neq 0^n}|1\rangle\,|y\rangle\otimes\left(\frac{1}{\sqrt{2^n}}\sum_b\widehat{\Delta f_b}(y)\,|b\rangle\right)$$

Suppose, we denote the normalized state $\frac{1}{\sqrt{\sigma_f}}\sum_b\Delta f(b)\,|b\rangle$ by $|\Phi'\rangle$ and the state $\frac{1}{\sqrt{2^n}}\sum_b\widehat{\Delta f_b}(y)\,|b\rangle$ by $\left|\Phi_y''\right\rangle$. We will rewrite the above superposition using these states and Eq. 4.2:

$$|\Phi\rangle = \sqrt{\frac{\sigma_f}{2^n}}\,|1\rangle\otimes|0^n\rangle\otimes|\Phi'\rangle + \sum_{y\neq 0^n}|1\rangle\,|y\rangle\left|\Phi_y''\right\rangle.$$

We immediately see that that the probability of observing $R_1$ in the state $|1\rangle$ and $R_2$ in the state $|0^n\rangle$ is exactly $\sigma_f/2^n$. This is where amplitude amplification comes in. To improve the probability to $1-\delta$ the number of Grover iterates that is required is $O(\frac{2^{n/2}}{\sqrt{\sigma_f}}\log\frac{2}{\delta})$. This translates to the same number of calls to the circuit in Fig. 4.4 which, in turn, implies that the number of calls to $U_f$ also follows the same asymptotic bound since the circuit calls $U_f$ only twice. It can be quickly verified from Fig. 4.4 that the circuit uses $\Theta(n)$ gates; therefore, the total number of gates used to implement Algorithm 4.1 is $O\left(n\frac{2^{n/2}}{\sqrt{\sigma_f}}\log\frac{2}{\delta}\right)$.

The amplification step will ensure that the amplitude of the state $|1\rangle|0^n\rangle|\Phi'\rangle$ is at least $\sqrt{1-\delta}$. Therefore, after amplification, $R_3$ will be in the state $|\Phi'\rangle$ with probability at least $1-\delta$, and when that happens, the observed state upon measuring $R_3$ would be some $|b\rangle$ with probability $\Delta f(b)^2/\sigma_f$—that is, a sample from the autocorrelation distribution as promised.

The Qiskit code that implements Algorithm 4.2 is as below. The function of interest here is $f(x) = x_1 \oplus x_1x_2 \oplus x_1x_2x_3 \oplus x_1x_2x_3x_4$.

```
1  #Importing the required classes and modules
2  from qiskit import *
3  from qiskit.circuit.library import *
4
5  #Defining the oracle for the function f(x)=x1+x1x2+
       x1x2x3+x1x2x3x4
6  def oracle():
7      circ = QuantumCircuit(4)
8      circ.z(0)
9      circ.cz(0,1)
10     circ.append(ZGate().control(2),range(3))
11     circ.append(ZGate().control(3),range(4))
12     return circ
13
14 #Defining a function that constructs and returns a
15 #quantum circuit for obtaining the Walsh distribution
16 #of the first order derivative
17 def ac_circ():
18     qc = QuantumCircuit(2*n)
19     qc.h(range(2*n))
20     qc.append(oracle(),range(n))
21     qc.cx(range(n,2*n),range(n))
22     qc.append(oracle(),range(n))
23     qc.cx(range(n,2*n),range(n))
24     qc.h(range(n))
25
26     return qc
27
28 #Defining the Grover iterate
29 def grover_iterate(n):
30     qc = QuantumCircuit(2*n)
31     qc.x(-1)
32     qc.append(ZGate().control((2*n)-1,ctrl_state='0'
       *((2*n)-1)), range(2*n))
33     qc.x(-1)
34     qc.append(ac_circ().inverse(),range(2*n))
35     qc.x(-1)
36     qc.append(ZGate().control((2*n)-1,ctrl_state='0'
       *((2*n)-1)), range(2*n))
37     qc.x(-1)
```

```
38      qc.append(ac_circ(),range(2*n))
39
40      return qc
41
42  #Defining the size of the input to the Boolean
43  #function f(x)
44  n = 4
45
46  #Measuring the first n qubits
47  qc = QuantumCircuit(2*n,2*n)
48  qc.append(ac_circ(),range(2*n))
49  for i in range(2):
50      qc.append(grover_iterate(n),range(2*n))
51
52  for i in range(2*n):
53      qc.measure(i,2*n-i-1)
54
55  #Executing the quantum circuit in a simulator
56  backend = Aer.get_backend('qasm_simulator')
57  shots = 8000
58  job = execute(qc,backend,shots=shots)
59  counts = job.result().get_counts()
60
61  #Constructing the list of the estimates of the
62  #First-Order Walsh derivatives at the point a
63  num0 = 0
64  for i in counts:
65      if i[:4]=='0000':
66          num0+=counts[i]
67  print("The number of time 0000 was observed on
          measuring the first 4 qubits is : ", num0, "\n")
68
69  wd = []
70  tot_counts = 0
71  for i in range(2**n):
72      ind = '0'*n + bin(i)[2:].zfill(n)
73      if ind in counts:
74          wd.append(counts[ind])
75          tot_counts+=counts[ind]
76      else:
77          wd.append(0)
78  print("The autocorrelation spectrum of f(x) is
          proportional to : ")
79  print([round(k/tot_counts,5) for k in wd])
```

**Listing 4.5** Qiskit code for autocorrelation sampling

```
1  Output:
2  The number of time 0000 was observed on measuring the
      first 4 qubits is :   7375
3
4  The autocorrelation spectrum of f(x) is proportional
      to :
```

5  [0.98346,  0.0042,  0.00339,  0.00393,  0.00041,  0.00054,
        0.00014,  0.00041,  0.00041,  0.00027,  0.00054,
        0.00027,  0.00027,  0.00054,  0.00068,  0.00054]

In Listing 4.5, we primarily define three different functions. As usual the oracle() function returns the oracle circuit for the given function which in this case is $f(x) = x_1 \oplus x_1 x_2 \oplus x_1 x_2 x_3 \oplus x_1 x_2 x_3 x_4$. The function ac_circ() creates a generic quantum circuit such that on providing the quantum circuit with an equal superposition of $n$ qubits as the first $n$ qubits and some $n$-bit pattern $a$ as the second $n$ qubits, returns a final state $|\psi\rangle$. The state $|\psi\rangle$ is such that the amplitudes of a basis states correspond to the Walsh coefficient of the first order derivative of $f(x)$ at the point $a$. The function grover_iterate() takes as input n and returns a quantum circuit that corresponds to the Grover's iterate to amplify the amplitude of the state $|0^n\rangle$. We then create a quantum circuit and use ac_circ() function to obtain the state of the circuit as $\frac{1}{\sqrt{2^n}} \sum_{x \in \{0,1\}^n} \sum_{b \in \{0,1\}^n} \widehat{\Delta f_b}(y) |y\rangle |b\rangle$. Next, we use the circuit returned by grover_iterate() to amplify the probability of obtaining 0000 on measuring the first 4 qubits and then measure the states. Thereafter, we execute the circuit in a simulator and return an array where the $i$th element of the array is the proportion of the string $i$ in the obtained output. We also return the number of times 0000 was observed on measuring the first 4 qubits. It is worth noticing that on changing the number of application of the Grover's iterate the frequency of observing 0000 in the first 4 qubits will change.

As from the output, it is clear that the amplification is nearly-optimal; we obtain the required state of $|0000\rangle$ about 7375 times out of the 8000 total shots.

## 4.3  Autocorrelation Estimation

The final problem that we discuss in this chapter is to estimate the value of $\Delta f(a)^2$ for any given $a \in \{0, 1\}^n$. An accurate estimate of this value can be used to further estimate the absolute value of $\Delta f(a)$; hence, we seek to perform the former task with a high accuracy, say, $\epsilon$ and a low probability of error, say $\delta$. The objective will be to compute some $\alpha \in [0, 1]$ such that

$$\Pr[\alpha - \epsilon \leq \Delta f(a)^2 \leq \alpha + \epsilon] \geq 1 - \delta$$

by making a few queries to $U_f$.

We use yet another magical technique available to quantum algorithm designers—quantum amplitude estimation or amplitude estimation in short. Suppose that there is some (classical or quantum) process whose output values, coming from some domain $D$, is probabilistic; let $\{p(x)\}_{x \in D}$ denote the probability distribution of its output values. Consider the task of computing, or estimating, $p(x)$ for a particular $x$. The standard way to solve this, using classical methods, is to run the process lots of times, say $N$ times, and observe in how many of them $x$ is output—let $m_x$ be

**Fig. 4.5** Swap-gate (left) and quantum circuit for swap-test (right)

that number. It is a basic fact in statistics that $p(\hat{x}) = \frac{m_x}{N}$ is a good and unbiased estimator of $p(x)$; in fact, $\mathbb{E}[p(\hat{x})] = p(x)$, and furthermore, $p(\hat{x})$ is within $\pm\epsilon$ of $p(x)$ with probability at least $1 - \delta$ if $N$ is chosen as $\frac{c}{\epsilon^2} \log \frac{1}{\delta}$ (here $c$ is a small constant that can be easily calculated using the Chernoff-Hoeffding's bound). Amplitude estimation is a quantum technique that too returns an estimate, denoted $\tilde{p}(x)$, within $\pm\epsilon$ with probability at least $1 - \delta$ and just makes $O\left(\frac{\pi}{\epsilon} \log \frac{1}{\delta}\right)$ calls to the process (implemented as an unitary operator).

An immediate strategy would be to express $\Delta f(a)$ or $\Delta f(a)^2$ as the expectation of a binary variable. Indeed, autocorrelation coefficient at $a$ can be expressed as the expectation of a $\pm 1$-valued random variable in the following manner.

$$\Delta f(a) = \frac{1}{2^n} \sum_x (-1)^{f(x)} (-1)^{f(x \oplus a)} = \mathbb{E}_x[(-1)^{f(x) \oplus f(x \oplus a)}]$$

Here, $x$ is chosen uniformly at random from $\{0, 1\}^n$. This expectation can be estimated using classical sampling, essentially an adaptation of the method described above to $\pm 1$-random variables; the number of samples needed, which is same as the number of calls to $f()$, is $O(\frac{1}{\epsilon^2} \log \frac{1}{\delta})$.

As before, the quest is to improve this bound by designing a quantum algorithm. The algorithm we describe next does exactly that by making $\Theta\left(\frac{\pi}{\epsilon} \log \frac{1}{\delta}\right)$ calls to $U_f$, almost a square-root improvement over the classical complexity. The main idea it uses is to generate a state with a probability that is related to $\Delta f(a)^2$ which can then be subjected to amplitude estimation. And this state will be generated with the help of the circuit for the "quantum swap test"—something which has no classical analogue.

Suppose we have two registers over the same number of qubits that are in states denoted by $|\psi\rangle$ and $|\phi\rangle$. The swap test circuit, denoted by $ST$ and illustrated in Fig. 4.5, uses an additional qubit initialized to $|0\rangle$ and applies a conditional swap-gate in a clever manner such that if the first (single-qubit) register is measured, then $|0\rangle$ is observed with probability $\frac{1}{2}[1 + |\langle\psi|\phi\rangle|^2]$. It is easy to show that the circuit performs the following transformation.

$$|0\rangle |\psi\rangle |\phi\rangle \xrightarrow{ST} |0\rangle \otimes \frac{1}{2}\Big[|\psi\rangle |\phi\rangle + |\phi\rangle |\psi\rangle\Big] + |1\rangle \otimes \frac{1}{2}\Big[|\psi\rangle |\phi\rangle - |\phi\rangle |\psi\rangle\Big]$$

Our algorithm for estimation of $\Delta f(a)^2$ is presented in Algorithm 4.2 and a circuit diagram is given in Fig. 4.6. We do not show the $|1\rangle$ qubit in the algorithm; it remains

**Require:** Parameters: $\epsilon$ (confidence), $\delta$ (error)
1: Start with four registers of which $R_1$ is initialized to $|a\rangle$, $R_2$ to $|0\rangle$, and $R_3, R_4$ to $|0^n\rangle$.
2: Apply these transformations.

$$|a\rangle\,|0\rangle\,|0^n\rangle\,|0^n\rangle$$
$$\xrightarrow{H^n \otimes H^n} |a\rangle\,|0\rangle\,\Big(\tfrac{1}{\sqrt{2^n}}\textstyle\sum_x |x\rangle\Big)\Big(\tfrac{1}{\sqrt{2^n}}\textstyle\sum_y |y\rangle\Big)$$
$$\xrightarrow{CNOT} |a\rangle\,|0\rangle\,\Big(\tfrac{1}{\sqrt{2^n}}\textstyle\sum_x |x\rangle\Big)\Big(\tfrac{1}{\sqrt{2^n}}\textstyle\sum_y |y \oplus a\rangle\Big)$$
$$\xrightarrow{U_f \otimes U_f} |a\rangle\,|0\rangle\,\Big(\tfrac{1}{\sqrt{2^n}}\textstyle\sum_x (-1)^{f(x)}|x\rangle\Big)\Big(\tfrac{1}{\sqrt{2^n}}\textstyle\sum_y (-1)^{f(y \oplus a)}|y \oplus a\rangle\Big)$$
$$\xrightarrow{CNOT} |a\rangle\,|0\rangle\,\Big(\tfrac{1}{\sqrt{2^n}}\textstyle\sum_x (-1)^{f(x)}|x\rangle\Big)\Big(\tfrac{1}{\sqrt{2^n}}\textstyle\sum_y (-1)^{f(y \oplus a)}|y\rangle\Big)$$
$$= |a\rangle\,|0\rangle\,|\psi\rangle\,|\phi_a\rangle$$

  – (Normalized state $\tfrac{1}{\sqrt{2^n}}\sum_x (-1)^{f(x)}|x\rangle$ is denoted $|\psi\rangle$)
  – (Normalized state $\tfrac{1}{\sqrt{2^n}}\sum_y (-1)^{f(y \oplus a)}|y\rangle$ is denoted $|\phi_a\rangle$)

3: Apply $ST$ on $R_2, R_3$ and $R_4$ to obtain

$$|a\rangle\left[\,|0\rangle \otimes \frac{1}{2}\big(|\psi\rangle\,|\phi_a\rangle + |\phi_a\rangle\,|\psi\rangle\big) + |1\rangle \otimes \frac{1}{2}\big(|\psi\rangle\,|\phi_a\rangle - |\phi_a\rangle\,|\psi\rangle\big)\right]$$

4: $\ell \leftarrow$ estimate probability of observing $R_2$ in the state $|0\rangle$ with accuracy $\pm\frac{\epsilon}{2}$ and error $\delta$
5: Return $2\ell - 1$ as the estimate of $|\Delta f(a)|^2$

**Algorithm 4.2:** Autocorrelation estimation at point $a$

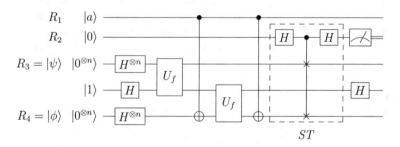

**Fig. 4.6**  Circuit for estimation of autocorrelation coefficient at a point $a$

in the state $|-\rangle$ throughout the circuit and its only role is to apply the $U_f$ gate as a phase-change operator:

$$U_f\,|x\rangle \mapsto (-1)^{f(x)}\,|x\rangle\,.$$

Steps 1, 2 and 3 of Algorithm 4.2 explain how we arrive at the state

$$|a\rangle\left[\,|0\rangle \otimes \frac{1}{2}\big(|\psi\rangle\,|\phi_a\rangle + |\phi_a\rangle\,|\psi\rangle\big) + |1\rangle \otimes \frac{1}{2}\big(|\psi\rangle\,|\phi_a\rangle - |\phi_a\rangle\,|\psi\rangle\big)\right]$$

in Step-3. Let $|\chi_a^0\rangle$ denote the state $\frac{1}{2}|\psi\rangle\,|\phi_a\rangle + \frac{1}{2}|\phi_a\rangle\,|\psi\rangle$. We will denote the probability of observing $R_2$ in the state $|0\rangle$ after Step-3 by $p_0$. Clearly, $p_0$ can be expressed as $\left\| |\chi_a^0\rangle \right\|^2$ which is

$$\left\||\chi_a^0\rangle\right\|^2 = \tfrac{1}{4}\left[2\||\psi\rangle\| \cdot \||\phi_a\rangle\| + 2|\langle\psi|\phi_a\rangle|^2\right] = \tfrac{1}{2}\left[1 + |\langle\psi|\phi_a\rangle|^2\right]$$

Further, observe that $\langle\psi|\phi\rangle = \tfrac{1}{2^n}\sum_x(-1)^{f(x)}(-1)^{f(x\oplus a)} = \Delta f(a)$. Therefore, $p_0 = \tfrac{1}{2} + \tfrac{1}{2}\Delta f(a)^2$. At this point the algorithm uses the amplitude estimation algorithm to estimate $p_0$ with accuracy $\epsilon/2$ with probability at least $1 - \delta$; the estimate is denoted $\ell$ which satisfies the following bounds.

$$\ell - \tfrac{\epsilon}{2} \leq p_0 \leq \ell + \tfrac{\epsilon}{2}$$
$$2\ell - \epsilon \leq 2p_0 \leq 2\ell + \epsilon$$
$$2\ell - 1 - \epsilon \leq 2p_0 - 1 \leq 2\ell - 1 + \epsilon$$
$$(2\ell - 1) - \epsilon \leq \Delta f(a)^2 \leq (2\ell - 1) + \epsilon$$

This shows that $2\ell - 1$ is an $\epsilon$-accurate estimate of $\Delta f(a)^2$.

For analysing the number of queries to $U_f$, first observe that the circuit to obtain the state in Step-3 of the algorithm (see Fig. 4.6) uses only two calls to $U_f$. The amplitude estimation procedure shall make $\Theta\left(\tfrac{\pi}{\epsilon}\log\tfrac{1}{\delta}\right)$ calls to this circuit, giving a total of $\Theta\left(\tfrac{\pi}{\epsilon}\log\tfrac{1}{\delta}\right)$ calls to $U_f$.

The above theorem shows how to estimate $\Delta f(a)^2$ using a quantum algorithm that shows a quadratic speedup over a classical sampling-based algorithm.

Finally, we provide the Qiskit code to obtain the autocorrelation coefficient at the point $a = 0110$ of the Boolean function $f(x) = x_1 \oplus x_1x_2 \oplus x_1x_2x_3 \oplus x_1x_2x_3x_4$ using the Swap test method.

```
1  #Importing the required classes and modules
2  from qiskit import *
3  from qiskit.circuit.library import *
4  from itertools import chain
5
6  #Defining the oracle for the function f(x)=x1+x1x2+
      x1x2x3+x1x2x3x4
7  def oracle():
8      circ = QuantumCircuit(4)
9      circ.z(0)
10     circ.cz(0,1)
11     circ.append(ZGate().control(2),range(3))
12     circ.append(ZGate().control(3),range(4))
13     return circ
14
15 #Defining a function that implements swap test
16 def swap_test(n):
17     circ = QuantumCircuit(2*n+1)
18     circ.h(0)
19     for i in range(n):
20         circ.append(CSwapGate(),[0,i+1,n+i+1])
21     circ.h(0)
```

```
22        return circ
23
24 #Defining a function that returns a circuit which
25 #implements the autocorrelation estimation at the
26 #point a as defined in the Algorithm.
27 def ac_estim(n,a):
28     circ = QuantumCircuit(3*n+1,1)
29     for i in range(n):
30         if a[i]=='1':
31             circ.x(2*n+i)
32     circ.h(range(2*n))
33     circ.append(oracle(),range(n))
34     circ.cx(range(2*n,3*n),range(n,2*n))
35     circ.append(oracle(),range(n,2*n))
36     circ.cx(range(2*n,3*n),range(n,2*n))
37     circ.append(swap_test(n),chain(range(3*n,3*n+1),
      range(2*n)))
38     circ.measure(-1,0)
39
40     return circ
41
42 #Setting the size of input to the Boolean function
43 #f(x) as n and the point of estimation as a
44 n=4
45 a='0110'
46
47 #Executing the estimation circuit in simulator
48 backend = Aer.get_backend('qasm_simulator')
49 shots = 8000
50 job = execute(ac_estim(n,a),backend, shots=shots)
51 count = job.result().get_counts()
52
53 print("The estimate of the square of the
      autocorrelation coefficient of f(x) at a is :")
54 print(round(2*(count['0']/shots)-1,5))
```

**Listing 4.6** Qiskit code for autocorrelation estimation at a point a using swap test method

```
1 Output:
2 The estimate of the square of the autocorrelation
      coefficient of f(x) at a is :
3 0.05975
```

In regards to the code in Listing 4.6, we define three functions, namely, oracle(), swap_test() and ac_estim(). The function oracle() is defined exactly the same as in Listing 4.5. As for the swap_test() function, it takes a number n as input and returns a circuit that performs the swap test circuit for two n qubit states as in the circuit in Fig. 4.5. The ac_estim() function takes as input the size the given Boolean function as n and a point a at which we prefer to obtain the estimation of the autocorrelation coefficient of $f(x)$. The function in turn returns a circuit that conforms to the circuit in Fig. 4.6. We then run the circuit returned by `ac_estim()` on giving the inputs $n = 4$ and $a = 0110$ in a simulator and obtain the result. Finally, we return $(2 * p_0) - 1$ as the estimate of the square of the autocorrelation coefficient of the function $f(x)$ where $p_0$ is the fraction of the output that was observed as 0.

## 4.4   Additional Implications

The autocorrelation spectrum is further used to define many characteristics of Boolean functions. We talk about a few direct applications. The absolute indicator of a function $f(x)$ is defined as the maximum value among the autocorrelation coefficients over all non-zero points. Mathematically, the absolute indicator of $f(x)$ is written as

$$\Delta(f) = \max_{a \in \{0,1\}^n, a \neq 0^{\otimes n}} |\Delta_f(a)|.$$

Similar to the concept of resiliency in the context of Walsh transform, here too we have a concept called propagation criteria. A Boolean function $f(x)$ is said to satisfy the propagation criteria of order $k$ if it holds that

$$\Delta_f(a) = 0 \text{ for } 1 \leq wt(a) \leq k.$$

A function is said to satisfy the strict avalanche criteria if the function $f(x)$ is such that $\Delta_f(a) = 0$ for all $a$ of weight 1. Further, the function $f(x)$ is said to satisfy the strict avalanche criteria of order $k$ if all the sub-functions obtained from $f(x)$ by fixing any $k$ input bits of $f(x)$ as some constants satisfy the strict avalanche criteria.

The algorithms related to autocorrelation spectra that were discussed in this chapter may prove to be useful for designing efficient quantum algorithms for these cryptographically significant properties of Boolean functions.

## Further Reading

Simon proposed the celebrated algorithm for a problem on Boolean functions now known as Simon's problem [7] which acted as a proof that quantum algorithms can provide exponential speedup over a classical computation. It should be noted that Grover's algorithm [4], the most employed tool in the previous chapter, can only provide a much slower quadratic speedup. Also it is to be noted that the Simon's algorithm works on a vectorial Boolean function. This might be interesting to note that the present day quantum computers are quite noisy (error-prone) and obtaining perfect results are elusive. In this regard, several modifications of the algorithms are studied towards better performance and one may refer to [6] for study and improvement over Simon's algorithm in a noisy quantum environment.

Further, we concentrate on $n$-input one output Boolean functions. The algorithms related to the autocorrelation coefficients and spectra were proposed recently by the authors [1]. These algorithms employ the concept of higher order derivatives of Boolean functions that was introduced by Lai [5] and used a combination of the Deutsch-Jozsa algorithm [3] and the techniques of amplitude amplification and estimation that were proposed by Brassard et al. [2].

# References

1. Bera, D., Maitra, S., Tharrmashastha, S.: Efficient quantum algorithms related to autocorrelation spectrum. In: International Conference on Cryptology in India 2019. LNCS, vol. 11898, pp. 415–432. Springer
2. Brassard, G., Hoyer, P., Mosca, M., Tapp, A.: Quantum amplitude amplification and estimation. Contemp. Math. **305**, 53–74 (2002)
3. Deutsch, D., Jozsa, R.: Rapid solution of problems by quantum computation. Proc. R. Soc. Lond., Ser. A **439**, 553–558 (1992)
4. Grover, L.K.: A fast quantum mechanical algorithm for database search. In: Proceedings of the Twenty-Eighth Annual ACM Symposium on Theory of Computing, vol. 1, pp. 212–219 (1996)
5. Lai, X.: Higher Order Derivatives and Differential Cryptanalysis. SECS, vol. 276, pp. 227–233. Springer, Boston (1994)
6. May, A., Schlieper, L., Schwinger, J.: Noisy Simon Period Finding (2019). https://arxiv.org/abs/1910.00802
7. Simon, D.R.: On the power of quantum computation. SIAM J. Comput. **26**(5), 1474–83 (1997)

# Chapter 5
# Conclusion and Research Direction

**Abstract** In this concluding chapter, we briefly revisit what we have studied in this book and then outline the recent state-of-the-art results related to quantum cryptanalysis of symmetric ciphers.

**Keywords** Autocorrelation spectrum · Boolean functions · Bernstein-Vazirani algorithm · CHSH game · Deutsch and Deutsch-Jozsa algorithm · Entanglement · Grover's algorithm · IBM Quantum · Qiskit · Measurement · No-cloning · Qubits · Quantum gates · Simon's algorithm · Superposition · Teleportation · Walsh transform

## 5.1 What Is Covered?

The keywords of this chapter in alphabetic order, i.e., Autocorrelation Spectrum, Boolean Functions, Bernstein-Vazirani Algorithm, CHSH Game, Deutsch and Deutsch-Jozsa Algorithm, Entanglement, Grover's Algorithm, IBM Quantum, Qiskit, Measurement, No-Cloning, Qubits, Quantum Gates, Simon's Algorithm, Superposition, Teleportation and Walsh Transform, provide an outline of what has been covered in this book.

In the first chapter, we presented introductory material on quantum information theory that covered the basic ideas of qubits, entanglement, measurement, superposition, no-cloning, teleportation and the CHSH game. We introduced the IBM Quantum environment early and presented Qiskit codes in this regard. Such codes are present in all the chapters in this book towards implementation of the the theoretical contents.

In the second chapter, we introduced the basic ideas of Boolean functions, the related cryptographic properties and their implementations as quantum circuits as well as, as Qiskit codes. The Deutsch-Jozsa algorithm and its relationship with the Walsh transformation is the theme of this chapter. The Deutsch and the Bernstein-Vazirani algorithms are also presented along-with.

The third chapter considers the Grover's algorithm. The main idea here is amplitude amplification which is the central idea behind Grover's algorithm. This is further exploited to study the Walsh spectrum of a Boolean function with greater details.

T. SAPV et al., *Quantum Algorithms for Cryptographically Significant Boolean Functions*, SpringerBriefs in Computer Science, https://doi.org/10.1007/978-981-16-3061-3_5

Quantum algorithms to evaluate the cryptographic properties like nonlinearity and resiliency are studied in this chapter. One may note that the Walsh spectrum takes care of 'confusion' that is required to be infused in a symmetric cipher.

Simon's algorithm is quite well known in studying the period of a Boolean function. This we explain in Chap. 4. In a similar direction, another important property in cipher design is 'diffusion' and the autocorrelation spectrum of a Boolean function is the related tool. We discuss quantum algorithms to study the Walsh spectra of autocorrelation spectrum and the higher order derivatives of a Boolean function.

While the first and the second chapters mostly cover some fundamental topics of quantum information and computation, the third and the fourth chapters, in addition to some basic materials, contain some recent research results. For further reading, in the next section, we refer to some very recent results in the domain of quantum cryptanalysis of symmetric ciphers.

## 5.2   Recent Results

It is  well known that the Shor's [23] algorithm has a devastating impact on classical public key cryptosystems that are based on factorization and discrete log. That is why there is a worldwide research effort to design public key cryptosystems that are resistant against any quantum adversary and a standardization process has also been initiated [21]. This is broadly known as Post Quantum Cryptography (PQC).

At the same time, Grover's algorithm [12] has serious implications against security of symmetric ciphers. Given a secret key of size $k$ bits, for an ideal cipher, the only attack in the classical domain is the exhaustive search that requires $O(2^k)$ complexity. However, generic application of Grover's search reduces this to $O(\sqrt{2^k})$ i.e., $O(2^{\frac{k}{2}})$. Thus, the effective security of the secret key length is reduced by half. This applies to any block or stream cipher and also provides a faster method in finding the pre-image of a hash function. However, this generic application of Grover's algorithm requires implementation of the cipher in quantum domain and then all the Grover's iterations would add to the circuit size. That is, considering a 256-bit secret key, the circuit size will be of the order of $2^{128}$ multiplied by the circuit size at each step. This is in fact huge, and thus given the present Noisy Intermediate-Scale Quantum (NISQ) technology [22], the attacks may not work perfectly in practice. Nevertheless, NIST has put a guideline on when such a cipher will be considered at risk [20], and roughly explains the size and depth of the quantum circuit. In this regard, one may refer to the works [1–3, 15, 24] to understand the circuit requirements for different kinds of quantum cryptanalysis.

Note that other than the generic attacks, it is also important to study different classes of symmetric key algorithms and hash functions with additional focus given on quantum adversaries. In this direction, some important quantum cryptanalytic results on hash functions are available in [9, 10, 13, 14]. Mostly Grover's and Simon's algorithms are revised and exploited in the initial study on quantum cryptanalysis [16–18]. Then, there are q series of recent works as evident from [4–7]. The

$k$-xor and $k$-xor-sum algorithms (related to generalized birthday problem) are combinatorially interesting and they are used in different cryptanalytic tools. Quantum solutions of these problems have been studied in [11, 19]. In the other direction, design of "lightweight symmetric ciphers secure against quantum adversaries" is also being considered with a serious effort [8]. The papers listed at the end of this chapter contains many of the state-of-the-art results at the time of writing this book.

# References

1. Anand, R., Maitra, A., Mukhopadhyay, S.: Grover on Simon. Quantum Inf. Process. **19**(9), 340 (2020)
2. Anand, R., Maitra, A., Mukhopadhyay, S.: Evaluation of Quantum Cryptanalysis on SPECK. INDOCRYPT. LNCS. Springer, Berlin (2020)
3. Anand, R., Maitra, S., Maitra, A., Mukherjee, C., Mukhopadhyay, S.: Resource estimation of Grovers-kind quantum cryptanalysis against FSR based symmetric ciphers (2020). https://eprint.iacr.org/2020/1438
4. Bonnetain, X., Naya-Plasencia, M.: Hidden Shift Quantum Cryptanalysis and Implications. ASIACRYPT (1), LNCS, vol. 11272, pp. 560–592. Springer (2018)
5. Bonnetain, X., Naya-Plasencia, M., Schrottenloher, A.: Quantum security analysis of AES. IACR Trans. Sym. Cryptol. **2019**(2), 55–93 (2019)
6. Bonnetain, X., Hosoyamada, A., Naya-Plasencia, M., Sasaki, Y., Schrottenloher, A.: Quantum Attacks Without Superposition Queries: The Offline Simon's Algorithm. ASIACRYPT (1). LNCS, vol. 11921, pp. 492–519. Springer (2019)
7. Bonnetain, X., Naya-Plasencia, M., Schrottenloher, A.: On Quantum Slide Attacks. SAC 2019. LNCS, vol. 11959, pp. 492–519. Springer, Berlin (2019)
8. Canteaut, A., Duval, S., Leurent, G., Naya-Plasencia, M., Perrin, L., Pornin, T., Schrottenloher, A.: Saturnin: a suite of lightweight symmetric algorithms for post-quantum security. IACR Trans. Sym. Cryptol. **2020**(S1), 160–207 (2020)
9. Chailloux, A., Naya-Plasencia, M., Schrottenloher, A.: An Efficient Quantum Collision Search Algorithm and Implications on Symmetric Cryptography. ASIACRYPT (2). LNCS, vol. 10625, pp. 211–240. Springer, Berlin (2017)
10. Dong, X., Sun, S., Shi, D., Gao, F., Wang, X., Hu, L.: Quantum Collision Attacks on AES-like Hashing with Low Quantum Random Access Memories. ASIACRYPT. LNCS. Springer, Berlin (2020)
11. Grassi, L., Naya-Plasencia, M., Schrottenloher, A.: Quantum Algorithms for the $k$-xor Problem. ASIACRYPT (1). LNCS, vol. 11272, pp. 527–559. Springer (2018)
12. Grover, L.K.: A fast quantum mechanical algorithm for database search. In: Proceedings of the Twenty-Eighth Annual ACM Symposium on Theory of Computing, pp. 212–219 (1996)
13. Hosoyamada, A., Sasaki, Y.: Finding Hash Collisions with Quantum Computers by Using Differential Trails with Smaller Probability than Birthday Bound. EUROCRYPT (2). LNCS, vol. 12106, pp. 249–279. Springer, Berlin (2020)
14. Hosoyamada, A., Yamakawa, T.: Finding Collisions in a Quantum World. Quantum Black-Box Separation of Collision-Resistance and One-Wayness. ASIACRYPT. LNCS. Springer, Berlin (2020)
15. Jaques, S., Naehrig, M., Roetteler, M., Virdia, F.: Implementing Grover Oracles for Quantum Key Search on AES and LowMC. EUROCRYPT (2). LNCS, vol. 12106, pp. 280–310. Springer, Berlin (2020)
16. Kaplan, M., Leurent, G., Leverrier, A., Naya-Plasencia, M.: Breaking Symmetric Cryptosystems Using Quantum Period Finding. CRYPTO (2). LNCS, vol. 9815, pp. 207–237. Springer, Berlin (2016)

17. Kaplan, M., Leurent, G., Leverrier, A., Naya-Plasencia, M.: Quantum differential and linear cryptanalysis. IACR Trans. Sym. Cryptol. **2016**(1), 71–94 (2016)
18. Leander, G., May, A.: Grover Meets Simon – Quantumly Attacking the FX-construction. ASIACRYPT (2). LNCS, vol. 10625, pp. 161–178. Springer, Berlin (2017)
19. Naya-Plasencia, M., Schrottenloher, A.: Optimal Merging in Quantum $k$-xor and $k$-xor-sum Algorithms. EUROCRYPT (2). LNCS, vol. 12106, pp. 311–340. Springer, Berlin (2020)
20. NIST. Submission requirements and evaluation criteria for the post-quantum cryptography standardization process (2016). https://csrc.nist.gov/CSRC/media/Projects/Post-Quantum-Cryptography/documents/call-for-proposals-final-dec-2016.pdf
21. NIST. Post-quantum cryptography. https://csrc.nist.gov/Projects/post-quantum-cryptography
22. Preskill, J.: Quantum computing in the NISQ era and beyond (2018). https://arxiv.org/abs/1801.00862
23. Shor, P.W.: Algorithms for quantum computation: discrete logarithms and factoring. In: Proceedings 35th Annual Symposium on Foundations of Computer Science, pp. 124–134. IEEE (1994)
24. Zou, J., Wei, Z., Sun, S., Liu, X., Wu, W.: Quantum Circuit Implementations of AES with Fewer Qubits. ASIACRYPT. LNCS. Springer, Berlin (2020)

# Index

© The Author(s), under exclusive license to Springer Nature Singapore Pte Ltd. 2021
T. SAPV et al., *Quantum Algorithms for Cryptographically Significant Boolean Functions*,
SpringerBriefs in Computer Science,
https://doi.org/10.1007/978-981-16-3061-3

Printed in the United States
by Baker & Taylor Publisher Services